Teacher's Guide

PATHWAYS

Reading, Writing, and Critical Thinking

3

Mari Vargo
Laurie Blass
Ingrid Wisniewska

NATIONAL GEOGRAPHIC LEARNING | HEINLE CENGAGE Learning

Australia • Brazil • Japan • Korea • Mexico • Singapore • Spain • United Kingdom • United States

Pathways 3 Teacher's Guide

Publisher: Andrew Robinson
Executive Editor: Sean Bermingham
Contributing Editor: Jennifer Monaghan
Development Editor: Karen Davy
Director of Global Marketing: Ian Martin
Marketing Manager: Emily Stewart
Director of Content and Media Production: Michael Burggren
Sr. Content Project Manager: Daisy Sosa
Manufacturing Buyer: Marybeth Hennebury
Cover Design: Page 2 LLC
Cover Image: Skip Brown/National Geographic
Interior Design: Page 2 LLC, Cenveo® Publisher Services/Nesbitt Graphics, Inc.
Composition: Cenveo Publisher Services

ISBN-13: 978-1-133-31739-5

ISBN-10: 1-133-31739-1

National Geographic Learning
20 Channel Center St.
Boston, MA 02210
USA

Cengage Learning is a leading provider of customized learning solutions with office locations around the globe, including Singapore, the United Kingdom, Australia, Mexico, Brazil, and Japan. Locate your local office at: **international.cengage.com/region**

Cengage Learning products are represented in Canada by Nelson Education, Ltd.

Visit National Geographic Learning online at **ngl.cengage.com**
Visit our corporate website at **www.cengage.com**

Printed in the United States of America
1 2 3 4 5 6 7 8 15 14 13

TABLE OF CONTENTS

Advantages of *Pathways Reading, Writing, and Critical Thinking*

In *Pathways Reading, Writing, and Critical Thinking*, real-world content from *National Geographic* publications provides a context for meaningful language acquisition. Students learn essential, high-frequency vocabulary, review important grammatical structures, and practice reading and writing skills that will allow them to succeed in academic settings.

Pathways Reading, Writing, and Critical Thinking can be used in a wide variety of language-learning programs, from high schools and community colleges to private language institutes and intensive English programs. The high-interest content motivates students and teachers alike.

The following features are included in *Pathways Reading, Writing, and Critical Thinking*:

- Academic Pathways goals at the beginning of each unit give students and teachers clear performance objectives.
- Opening pages introduce the unit theme and provide key vocabulary and concepts.
- Readings in a variety of academic content areas and genres present target vocabulary and provide ideas for writing.
- An audio program includes recordings of all the reading texts.
- Clear grammar charts present key structures and language for writing assignments.
- An *Independent Student Handbook* and Vocabulary Index serve as tools to use in class or for self-study and review.

Teaching Language Skills and Academic Literacy

Students need more than language skills to succeed in an academic setting. In addition to teaching the English language, the *Pathways* series teaches academic literacy, which includes not only reading, writing, speaking, and listening skills, but also visual literacy, classroom participation and collaboration skills, critical thinking, and the ability to use technology for learning. Students today are expected to be motivated, inquisitive, original, and creative. In short, they're expected to possess quite an extensive skills set before they even begin their major course of study.

Using *National Geographic* Content in a Language Class

The use of high-interest content from real *National Geographic* publications sets the *Pathways* series apart. Students are engaged by fascinating stories about real people and places around the world and the important issues that affect us all.

High-interest reading passages provide opportunities to practice reading and critical thinking skills, while providing vocabulary and ideas for writing assignments.

The topics in *Pathways Reading, Writing, and Critical Thinking* correspond to academic subject areas and appeal to a wide range of interests. For example:

Academic Subject Area	Unit Title	Unit Theme
Sociology	*City Solutions*	the global growth of cities and the positive aspects of urbanization
Earth Science	*Danger Zones*	coping with natural disasters and the causes of supervolcano eruptions
Economics/Business	*The Business of Tourism*	a definition of geotourism and examples of geotourism success stories
Health/Medicine	*Medical Innovators*	pioneers of medical innovation, past and present
Anthropology/Linguistics	*World Languages*	the future of English and other world languages, and efforts to preserve disappearing languages

Increasing Visual Literacy

Photographs, maps, charts, and graphs can all convey enormous amounts of information. Lecturers and professors rarely present information without some kind of visual aid. Helping students to make sense of visuals is an important part of preparing them for academic success.

Language Hot Spots

Hot spots are places where many languages are disappearing.

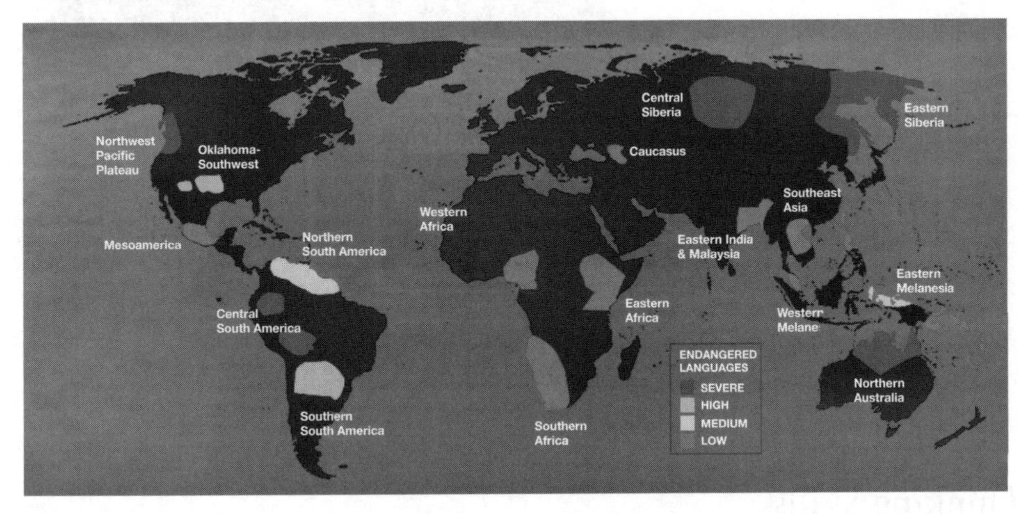

Maps are used in the *Pathways* series not only to show locations and geographical features, but also to illustrate historical facts and current trends—both local and global. In an academic setting, the ability to read maps is expected, and *Pathways* gives students opportunities to hone that skill.

Charts and graphs present numerical data in a visual way, and the *Pathways* series gives students practice in reading them.

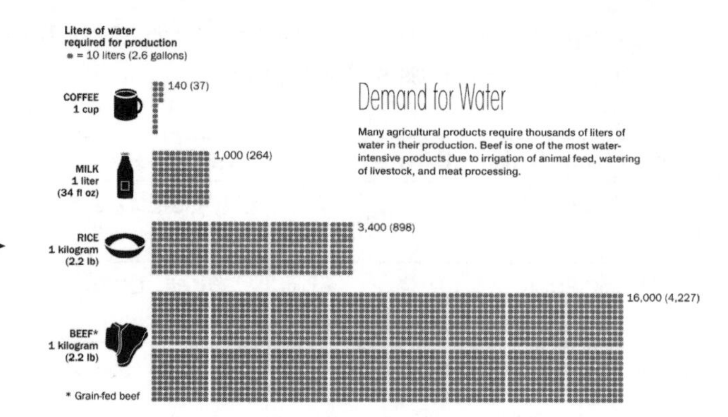

Pathways uses a variety of graphic organizers to present content. Graphic organizers appeal to visual learners by showing relationships between ideas in a visual way. Students use graphic organizers for a number of reading and writing tasks such as note taking, comparing similarities and differences, brainstorming, identifying main ideas and details, and organizing notes for writing assignments.

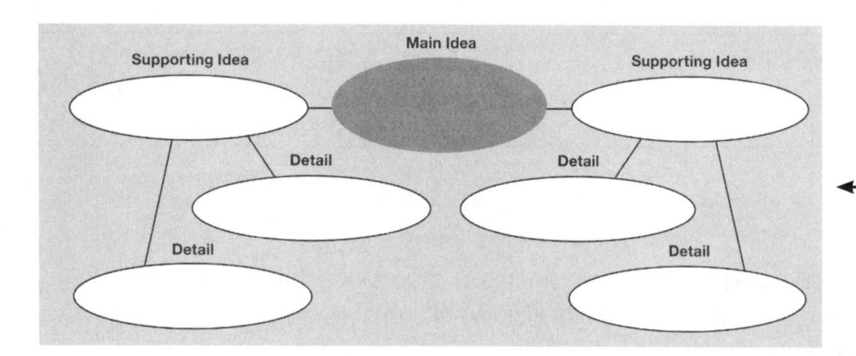

In addition to the more standard pie charts and bar graphs, *Pathways* includes other stimulating informational visuals from *National Geographic* publications.

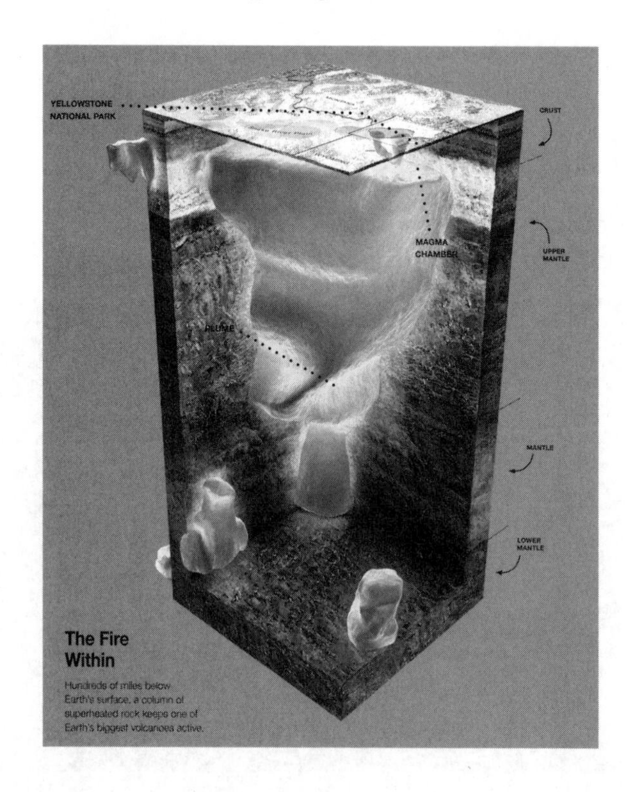

Building Critical Thinking Skills

Critical thinking skills are explicitly taught and practiced in *Pathways Reading, Writing, and Critical Thinking.* Critical thinking—the ability to make judgments and decisions based on evidence and reason—is an essential skill for students in an academic setting, where they're expected to reflect on and analyze information rather than simply remember it. Students need to be prepared to think critically while listening, reading, writing, and participating in discussions.

The ability to think critically also contributes to language acquisition by requiring deep processing of the language. Having to consider an idea in relation to other ideas and then articulate a response or an opinion about it, involves making complex associations in the brain. This thought process in turn leads to better comprehension and retention of the target language.

Here are just a few examples of the academic tasks that require critical thinking skills:

- deciding which material from a reading to take notes on
- determining a writer's purpose when assessing the content of a reading
- forming an opinion on an issue based on facts and evidence
- relating new information to one's personal experiences
- giving specific examples to support one's main idea
- evaluating sources of information
- synthesizing information

The *Pathways* series gives explicit instruction and practice of critical thinking skills. Each unit has a Critical Thinking Focus and several practice exercises. For example:

CT Focus

Writers may use **personal stories**, or **anecdotes**, to illustrate a theory or an idea. When you read about a personal experience, think about the writer's reason for including it. What theory or idea does it help illustrate?

D | **Critical Thinking: Analyzing and Inferring Purpose.** According to the writer, how were Asencio's and Pabon's reactions similar and different? Complete the Venn diagram with the six physical reactions (a–f). Then answer this question: Why do you think the author included anecdotes about Asencio and Pabon?

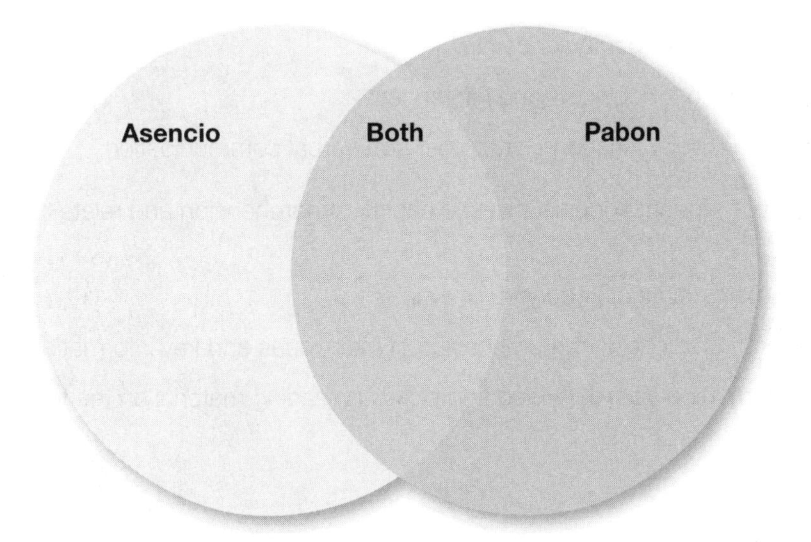

Using Video in the Language Classroom

The video clips in *Pathways Reading, Writing, and Critical Thinking* come from the award-winning *National Geographic* film collection and act as a bridge between Lessons A and B of each unit. The videos present another perspective on the unit theme in a visually dynamic way. The narration for each video has been carefully graded to feature vocabulary items and structures that are appropriate for students' proficiency level.

Teaching video-viewing skills

In daily life, nonfiction videos can be found on television, on the Internet, and in movie theaters in the form of documentaries. Just as *Pathways* provides a wide variety of reading passages to build students' reading skills, the series also builds viewing skills with videos from *National Geographic*. *Pathways* promotes visual and digital literacy so learners can competently use a wide range of modern media.

Videos differ from reading texts in important ways. First, students are processing information by viewing and listening simultaneously. Visual images include information about the video's setting as well as clues found in nonverbal communication, such as facial expressions, gestures, and other body language. The video may also include maps and diagrams to explain information and processes. The soundtrack contains narration, conversations, music, and sound effects. Some contextual words may appear on screen in signs or as identification of people or settings. In addition, full English subtitles are available as a teaching and learning option.

The Viewing section

The viewing section in each unit features activities for students to do before, while, and after they watch the video.

Before Viewing prepares students for the video by activating their background knowledge and stimulating interest in the topic. Some effective ways of previewing include

- brainstorming ideas and discussing what the class already knows about the topic;
- using photographs and the video's title to predict the content;
- pre-teaching key vocabulary essential to understanding the video content.

While Viewing tasks allow students to focus on

- checking their predictions;
- identifying the main ideas;
- watching and listening for particular details;
- watching and listening for opinions and inferences;
- observing gestures, body language, and other non-verbal communication.

After Viewing gives students opportunities to check comprehension and relate the video to other aspects of the unit by

- describing the main points or sequence of events;
- answering questions to check comprehension of main ideas and key information;
- synthesizing information from the video and previous reading material on the topic.

Some options for using the videos

Preview each video before presenting it in class to become familiar with the content, anticipate questions students might have, and plan how to exploit the video most effectively. See individual units in this Teacher's Guide for notes and suggestions for teaching each video.

Here are some techniques for using video in class:

- Have students preview the video by reading the transcript in the back of the student textbook.
- Pause, rewind, or fast-forward the video to focus on key segments or events.
- Pause the video and ask students to predict what will happen next. Resume the video so students can check their predictions.
- Have students watch the video, or parts of the video, with the sound off so they can focus on what they see. Have students share their ideas about the content. Then play the video with the sound on so students can check their ideas.
- After students have watched the video with the sound on, have them watch again with sound off. Pause the video in different places and ask students to retell the information in their own words.
- Have students watch first without subtitles and discuss the main ideas. Then play the video again with subtitles so students can check their ideas.
- Have students watch the video with the subtitles to help with unknown vocabulary and to aid comprehension.
- Have students watch the video independently and complete the activities in the Online Workbook.

As an optional special project, have students make a presentation or create a written report about a video of their choice, using language they have learned from the textbook and the video narration.

Video scripts are printed in the back of the student textbook. All video clips are on the Online Workbook, the Presentation Tool CD-ROM, and on the classroom DVD. The Online Workbook also contains additional activities about the video.

Features of the *Pathways* Teacher's Guide

The *Pathways* Teacher's Guide contains teaching notes, answer keys, reading and video overviews, and warm-up and extension activities to help teachers present the material in the student textbook.

Ideas for... Boxes

Throughout the *Pathways* Teacher's Guide, there are three types of *Ideas for*. . . Boxes:

- **Ideas for Presenting Grammar** provide a variety of ways to introduce grammatical structures and utilize the grammar charts presented in the Language for Writing sections of the textbook.
- **Ideas for Checking Understanding** present additional questions for assessing students' comprehension of the reading texts.
- **Ideas for Expansion** suggest ways to expand on the content of the book when students need extra instruction or when they have a high level of interest in a topic.

Tips

Tips for instruction and classroom management are provided throughout the *Pathways* Teacher's Guide. The tips are especially helpful to less-experienced teachers, but they are also a resource for more-experienced teachers, providing new ideas and adding variety to the classroom routine.

Suggested Time Frames

The main sections of Lessons A, B, and C in the Teacher's Guide contain small clock icons with suggested times for completing the various tasks. The Writing Task sections in Lesson C do not have time icons because students will likely do writing assignments independently, outside of class. The times are intended as suggestions and may vary, depending on particular teaching situations. Similarly, the estimated time for completing a unit is between four and five class hours. This estimate may vary, depending on how much material is presented in class, given as homework, or other factors.

Graphic Organizers

A set of ten graphic organizers is included in the back of the Teacher's Guide (pages 101–110). You can photocopy these organizers as optional ways to help students organize information as they read particular reading texts in the units.

Audio Program

The audio program includes recordings of all the reading passages in the student textbook. As an option, you may have students listen to the texts while they read.

Following are some frequently asked questions about the *Pathways Reading, Writing, and Critical Thinking* series, answered by authors Mari Vargo and Laurie Blass.

1. How are the Student Book units organized?

Each unit in the *Pathways Reading, Writing, and Critical Thinking* series consists of three lessons: A, B, and C. Lessons A and B focus on reading, and Lesson C on writing. A video viewing segment between Lessons A and B serves as a bridge between the two readings and offers another perspective on the unit theme. Together, these lessons take students from an introduction to the unit theme, through a series of structured reading, vocabulary, and critical thinking activities, and finally through a guided writing assignment that synthesizes the skills, topics, and language presented in the unit.

2. What is the purpose of the Opening and Exploring the Theme pages?

The Opening page presents the unit goals—the Academic Pathways—and provides a general introduction to the unit theme through discussion questions. Exploring the Theme pages are springboards for students to interact with photographs and other graphical information such as maps, graphs, and charts. These pages get students thinking critically and sharing ideas about the unit theme. They present each unit's key concepts and vocabulary while providing opportunities for students to develop visual literacy skills.

3. How are the Lesson A and B readings different?

The Lesson A and B readings present academic content in a variety of genres and formats, and offer different perspectives on the unit themes. This content is adapted from a variety of *National Geographic* sources such as print and online features and articles. The Lesson A readings are primarily single, linear texts. The Lesson B readings are usually a group of related shorter readings. They represent a variety of formats and text types, including news articles, Web pages, interviews, and profiles, that are linked to each other or to maps and other graphics. The linked aspect of the Lesson B reading texts mirrors a real-world, online reading experience.

4. How does *Pathways Reading, Writing, and Critical Thinking* develop reading strategies?

Each Lesson A presents an academic reading skill along with a series of practice activities. These skills include identifying main and supporting ideas, interpreting visual information, identifying sequence, scanning for specific information, and using graphic organizers to take notes. Students apply what they have learned to the Lesson A reading and then have an opportunity to reinforce the skill in the Lesson B reading. In addition, Strategy boxes appear in various places throughout a unit, wherever students will benefit from a reminder of a previously taught skill.

5. How does the series develop critical thinking skills?

Critical thinking skills are explicitly taught and practiced in *Pathways Reading, Writing, and Critical Thinking*. Each Lesson A includes a specific CT (critical thinking) Focus box that explains the skill—often modeling the thinking process required by the skill through a series of questions. Critical thinking skills include making inferences, evaluating sources for reliability, analyzing the function and purpose of a text, and relating information to personal experience. Students apply the skill to the reading passages in Lessons A and B. Additional CT Focus boxes appear in other places in a unit, wherever students might benefit from a reminder of the skill.

In addition, there are multiple opportunities throughout each unit for students to practice synthesizing information—relating and connecting ideas from different parts of the unit—an essential skill for academic success. Students synthesize and apply information from the video and the Lesson A and B readings, which also prepares them for the unit's writing assignment.

6. How does the series build vocabulary skills?

A set of academic and high-frequency vocabulary items is targeted in both Lessons A and B. Students acquire and reinforce their knowledge of these items by identifying them in context, guessing their meaning, and using them in activities that reinforce meaning and usage. These target words are reinforced and recycled throughout the series.

In addition, Word Partners and Word Link boxes in Lessons A and B expand students' working vocabulary. Word Partners boxes show high-frequency patterns, or collocations, in which target words appear. Word Link boxes focus on prefixes, suffixes, and roots associated with target words.

7. What is the writing process approach taken in this series?

In acquiring academic writing skills, students need to learn early on that writing is rewriting. This is the premise of the process approach to writing, and the approach taken by *Pathways Reading, Writing, and Critical Thinking*. Accordingly, as students work through the pre-writing, writing, and post-writing activities in each unit, they draft and re-draft their assignments. Repeating this process as they progress through the units, students internalize the steps and gradually become more independent writers.

8. How does it develop writing skills?

The writing section of each unit, Lesson C, begins with a presentation of the writing topic, and then proceeds through the writing process: gathering ideas, planning, drafting, revising, and editing. Students follow this process in a step-by-step manner, working through a series of structured activities. For example, they use outlines and graphic organizers in the planning stage, answer focused questions in the revision stage, and use a checklist in the editing stage.

Each Lesson C includes a Writing Skill presentation box along with a series of practice activities. These presentations include basic paragraph writing skills such as writing topic sentences and supporting main ideas. Later, students move to paragraph organization and development for a variety of genres such as describing, persuading, showing similarities and differences, and explaining a process. Students practice by evaluating model paragraphs, and then apply what they've learned to their own paragraphs as they write and revise their assignments.

In addition, each Lesson C includes a Language for Writing presentation that highlights a lexical or grammar point specifically useful for that unit's writing assignment. Examples include using the simple past for a descriptive paragraph, using *by* + gerund for a cause-effect paragraph, and using comparative adjectives for a comparison paragraph. Students practice the structure in an activity, and then apply what they've learned to their own paragraphs as they write and edit their work.

9. What are some things to keep in mind when using the writing process?

In the brainstorming stage, students work with partners. This helps them express and clarify their ideas before they begin to write. In this stage, remind students that they should not monitor themselves or each other in any way. That is, ideas should flow freely without criticism or limitation.

As part of the brainstorming stage, students write a journal entry in a timed, free-writing activity. This activity should be done in class, if possible, so you can time it. The journal activity is a fluency exercise—that is, the focus is on generating ideas. Accordingly, remind students not to worry about grammar, spelling, or punctuation. The goal is to record ideas in a fluent manner. Do not correct or grade journal entries. If you collect them, you may want to write supportive, constructive comments on students' ideas.

The editing phase includes a peer evaluation activity that encourages students to give each other positive feedback at the outset. Reinforce the idea that students should read their partner's draft first just for meaning and to find at least one positive thing to say about the ideas in the paragraph. If necessary, provide students with some positive conversation starters such as "I like the way you explain X." "Your idea about X is interesting." Remind them of some ways to soften suggestions, such as: "You might want to . . . " "You could . . . ".

10. How are reading and writing integrated in the series?

All the lessons in each unit of *Pathways Reading, Writing, and Critical Thinking* are thematically linked. Lesson A and B readings and activities present and reinforce vocabulary, language, and ideas that students will use in their Lesson C writing assignments. In addition, Lesson A and B readings and skill presentations often model the genre that students will be writing in Lesson C. For example, in Unit 5, students learn to identify cause and effect in the Lesson A passage, review the skill in Lesson B, and then write a cause-effect paragraph. In Unit 7, students identify the writer's tone and purpose in a Lesson A passage, review the skill in Lesson B, and then write a persuasive essay in Lesson C.

Social Relationships

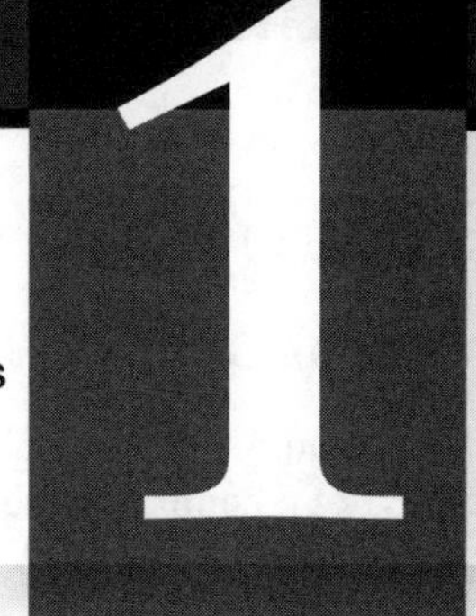

Academic Track	Academic Pathways:	
Interdisciplinary	Lesson A:	Identifying main and supporting ideas Evaluating supporting arguments
	Lesson B:	Understanding related science news reports
	Lesson C:	Reviewing paragraph writing Writing a comparison paragraph

Unit Theme

Unit 1 explores the topic of social and family relationships in the animal world, and compares some ways these relationships are similar to human social behavior.

Think and Discuss *(page 1)*

5 mins

- Ask students to describe the photo. How does the photo relate to the unit title?
- Ask: *What adjectives does the photo make you think of?* (Possible answers: caring, protective, nurturing, maternal)
- Use these answers to lead into a discussion of whether animals can feel emotions. What kind of emotions can they feel? (Possible answers: happiness, sadness, loneliness, trust, loyalty)
- Discuss question 1 as a class. Ask: *Do men and women have different roles in the family? In the workplace? In society? How are they different and what are the reasons for this?*
- For question 2, you may want to distinguish between roles that are based on physical differences and those that are socially constructed.

Exploring the Theme *(pages 2–3)*

15 mins

- The opening spread features a photo of tourists watching snow monkeys enjoying a hot spring in Japan.
- Ask students to describe the photo. Ask: *Where are they?* (At a volcanic hot spring in Japan) *What is the weather like? What are the tourists doing? Why? What are the monkeys doing? Why?*
- Ask students to read the information at the bottom of page 3. Check comprehension by asking: *What is a primate? What is a primatologist? Why are scientists interested in similarities between humans and nonhuman primates?*
- Have students discuss the three questions. Compare answers as a class. Ask students what characteristics they consider to be unique to humans.
- Note: Primates are the most highly evolved animal species and are characterized by large brains, binocular vision, the ability to use tools, the tendency to live in social groups, and the ability to communicate.

Answer Key

1. Gorillas, bonobos, orangutans, and chimpanzees
2. The ability to communicate, use tools, and live in social groups
3. Answers will vary.

IDEAS FOR . . . Expansion

Ask students to find out more about research on primates. What other characteristics have been found to be similar between humans and animals? Why is this important? What can we learn from this?

Preparing to Read *(page 4)*

30 mins

WARM-UP

The Lesson A target vocabulary is presented in the context of a comparison between office life and life in the jungle.

Ask students to tell you any personal anecdotes about conflicts or problems that they (or any friends or family) have experienced when working in an office. Share some of your own experiences with the class.

Exercise A. | Building Vocabulary

- Have students find the words in the reading and use the other words around them to guess their meanings.
- Do the first item together with the class as an example. Note that *function* is used as a verb, not as a noun.
- Check the answers by asking volunteers to read aloud a sentence each.
- Ask students for other word forms of each word. (Possible answers: functional, hierarchical, cooperative)

Answer Key

1. function	**6.** perception
2. hierarchy	**7.** conflict
3. dynamics	**8.** reveal
4. cooperate	**9.** status
5. role	**10.** distribution

TIP **Review some ways to use context to identify the meaning of target vocabulary. One way to approach this is to try replacing the target word with other similar words. For example, *People often have the perception that the animal world is full of conflict.* In this sentence, the word *perception* can be replaced by *idea, opinion,* or *impression.***

Exercise B. | Using Vocabulary

- After students discuss in pairs, invite volunteers to share their answers with the class.
- As an extension, ask students to make additional questions using other words from exercise A.
- Point out the **Word Partners** box. Encourage students to note word partnerships such as these when they record new words and expressions in their vocabulary notebooks.

Exercise C. | Brainstorming

- Invite a volunteer from each group to share their answers with the class.
- Pool what students know about animals that cooperate with each other. You may want to set this question as a homework journal task.

Answer Key

Possible answers:
It is less stressful.
Work is done more efficiently.
Bees, ants, and penguins cooperate with each other.

Exercise D. | Predicting

- Explain that *predicting* is trying to guess the gist, or general idea, of the reading passage.
- Encourage students to look at the title of the reading as well as the photos, captions, and subheads. This will help them predict what the passage is about.
- Students will check their predictions later, as they read the passage.

track **1-01**

Ask students to read the passage. You may want to have students listen to the audio as they read. Point out that the vocabulary definitions in the footnotes at the bottom of pages 5–7 will help them understand the reading.

IDEAS FOR . . . Expansion

Advise students to start a vocabulary notebook. Demonstrate on the board how to write new words in the notebook. Ask students for suggestions about what information to include. For example, they might include translations, example sentences, or collocations (words that commonly appear together).

Overview of the Reading

The passage examines ideas from the book *The Ape in the Corner Office: Understanding the Workplace Beast in All of Us* by science writer Richard Conniff. Research suggests that there are similarities in behavioral patterns between primates in the wild and humans in a corporate environment. While conflict and cooperation exist in both animal and human societies, the author concludes that in both cooperative activity is usually more prevalent and more beneficial than showing aggression.

Vocabulary Notes

Ask about or explain the meanings of these additional words in the reading.

mirror (paragraph A) = reflect, be similar to

ape (paragraph B) = name of a group of tailless primates that includes gorillas, chimpanzees, orangutans, and gibbons

corporate behavior (paragraph B) = behavior of employees in companies
key (paragraph B) = important, essential
assert (oneself) (paragraph B) = establish one's status or power
limited (paragraph C) = restricted
in the wild (paragraph C) = in a natural habitat
essentially (paragraph C) = basically
thrive (paragraph C) = do well
have a reputation for (paragraph C) = be known for
groom (paragraph C) = stroke, clean
get ahead (paragraph D) = advance
scheme (paragraph D) = plan
alliance (paragraph D) = friendship
rival (paragraph D) = competitor
relative (paragraph E) = depending on other factors
defer (to someone) (paragraph E) = obey someone because they have higher status
power drive (paragraph F) = determination to achieve something
pound (paragraph F) = beat, hit
screech (paragraph F) = let out a high-pitched scream
make the case (paragraph G) = argue, assert

IDEAS FOR . . . Checking Comprehension

Ask additional questions about the reading, or write them on the board.

1. How do the photos illustrate the points in the passage?
2. What popular perception of the animal world does the author contradict? (People think that it is full of conflict and aggression, but it is actually quite peaceful and harmonious most of the time.)
3. Give some examples of how friends might help you to get ahead in your career.
4. What are the advantages of hierarchies? What are the disadvantages?
5. What are some ways that managers can intimidate employees? Give some of your own examples.
6. According to the author, what is the long-term result of aggressive behavior? (It leads to isolation for the aggressor.) Do you agree?

45 mins

Understanding the Reading
(page 8)

Check students' predictions in exercise **D** on page 4.

Answer Key

1. Nonhuman primates (such as chimpanzees and baboons) and humans in an office/work environment
2. Similarities between these two groups

Exercise A. | Identifying Main Ideas

- First, ask students to look back at the passage and try to identify the four most important ideas. Discuss them briefly as a class.
- Then ask students to complete the first column in the chart.
- Draw the chart on the board and check the answers by asking students to tell you what to write in the first column.

Answer Key

1. live in harmony / conflict
2. similar social networking strategies
3. hierarchies
4. aggressive

Exercise B. | Identifying Key Details

- Explain that columns 2 and 3 give specific examples of the ideas in column 1.
- Allow time for students to complete the chart individually.
- Invite volunteers to come to the board to write their answers. Encourage others in the class to agree or disagree.

Answer Key

Human Examples	Primate Examples
b, g, h, l	b, f, g, h, l
c, d, e, i	d, e
a	m
j	k

Exercise C. | Identifying Supporting Ideas

- Explain that supporting ideas are additional information about key details.
- Ask students to review the passage and write their answers individually.
- Then have students discuss the answers in pairs.
- Check answers as a class.

Answer Key

1. Five percent / Paragraph C
2. When food is scarce / Paragraph E
3. It can result in isolation for the aggressor. / Paragraph F

Exercise D. | Critical Thinking: Evaluating Supporting Arguments

- Draw students' attention to the **CT Focus** box. Discuss why it is important to evaluate supporting arguments. Ask: *What kind of questions can help you to evaluate the writer's arguments?*
- Use the examples from the reading to practice evaluating. For example, the article provides a roughly equal amount of description of both human and ape behavior.
- Ask students to justify their answers by referring to points in the reading.

Exercise E. | Personalizing

- Have students discuss their ideas in pairs.
- You may want to ask each pair to choose a different statement in the reading and think of examples that support or contradict it.
- Write the following sentences on the board as a guide to help students present their ideas: *The passage states that . . . In my experience, this is true / not always true because . . .*

45 mins

Developing Reading Skills

(page 9)

Reading Skill: Identifying Main and Supporting Ideas

- Make sure students understand the difference between main and supporting ideas.
- Refer back to exercises A, B, and C on the previous page to illustrate the difference.
- Explain that understanding this difference is key to improving reading skills, understanding new information, and organizing information mentally and in your notes.
- Go over the information in the box. Have students reread paragraph C and tell you the main idea.

Exercise A. | Identifying Main Ideas

- Tell students to reread the relevant paragraphs in the passage and choose their answers.
- Allow time for them to discuss their answers with a partner.
- Ask volunteers to explain their choices to the class.
- As an extension, ask students to reread paragraphs B and G and identify the main idea in each.

Answer Key

1. a **2.** b **3.** b

Exercise B. | Applying

- To make this task more challenging, ask students to cover the sentences below the paragraph and try to identify the main idea by themselves.
- Check the answers as a class.
- Ask students to identify the three places where the main idea is restated.
- Ask students to explain how the supporting ideas relate to the main idea.
- Ask students to explain the final sentence. In what way does this behavior show that gorillas are adaptable, innovative, and intelligent?

Answer Key

(S) Male gorillas hit the water with their palms open.

(M) Male gorillas splash water to get the attention of females and to intimidate other males.

(S) Lowland gorillas go to swamps to eat and to meet other gorillas.

IDEAS FOR . . . Expansion

Ask students to write a summary of the reading passage on pages 5–7. This can be done in groups or individually for homework.

Then have students exchange their summaries. Have them underline the main ideas in red, underline the supporting ideas in blue, and draw a wavy line under any extra details.

Tell students to give each other feedback on their summaries. Were any main points left out? Could any details be omitted?

30 mins

Viewing: Elephant Orphans *(page 10)*

Overview of the Video

The video presents some insights into everyday life at the David Sheldrick Wildlife Trust in Kenya. This charity was set up in 1977 to take care of baby elephants whose mothers had been killed by poachers.

Vocabulary Notes

wildlife trust = a nature reserve that is set up and run by a charity to protect wild animals
poacher = a person who catches and kills animals illegally
caregiver / keeper = alternative name for caretaker, i.e., a person who takes care of the animals

Before Viewing

Exercise A. | Using a Dictionary

- Ask students to describe the photo. Ask: *What is special about these elephants? Why are they being fed with baby bottles?*
- Point out the globe and the location of Kenya. Ask: *What do you know about Kenya? What do you know about elephants in Africa? What do you think the purpose of a wildlife trust is?*
- Have students work in pairs to discuss the words and match them with their definitions.
- Compare answers as a class.

Answer Key

1. reintroduction **2.** caretakers **3.** slaughtered
4. maternal **5.** interaction **6.** orphan

Exercise B. | Thinking Ahead

- Explain that thinking ahead (or predicting) helps us to assimilate new information more easily.
- After students have a chance to talk with a partner, ask pairs to tell the class about their ideas.

Answer Key

Possible answers:

food, shelter, protection, affection

While Viewing

- Ask students to read the questions.
- Play the video while students write short answers to the questions as they watch.

Answer Key

1. 80 percent
2. A lot of care, attention, and interaction
3. They lie down with them, cover them with a blanket, play with them, and sleep with them.
4. Need to play, to have social interaction, to feel safe, . . . and they both like to be naughty sometimes

Vocabulary Notes

daybreak = sunrise, dawn
trial and error = trying one theory after another until the right answer is found
roam = wander
adolescent = teenager
periodically = from time to time

After Viewing

Exercise A.

- Have students work in pairs to discuss and compare answers.
- Play the video again and check answers.

Exercise B. | Critical Thinking: Synthesizing

- Tell students to look back at the reading passage on pages 5–7 about primates and their behavior.
- Students may want to create a Venn diagram to summarize their findings.

Answer Key

Possible answers:

Primates and elephants both live in social groups, have complex social and emotional relationships, and take care of each other; primate infants and elephant infants need maternal care in the early stages of their lives.

Note: More information about the David Sheldrick Wildlife Trust can be found here: http://www.sheldrickwildlifetrust.org/

IDEAS FOR . . . Checking Comprehension

Ask these additional questions about the video or write them on the board.

1. Where is the David Sheldrick Wildlife Trust located? (On the edge of Nairobi's National Park in Kenya)
2. What kind of milk do the elephants drink? (Baby formula, milk for human babies that is not made from cow's milk)
3. How much milk do they drink in a day? (24 pints)
4. What do they add to the milk after the elephant is six months old? (Dried coconut and cooked oatmeal porridge)
5. How many keepers are there? (51)
6. How long does it take to reintroduce an elephant to the wild? (Up to 10 years)
7. How many elephants are there in the wild in Africa today? (About 250,000)
8. Why are elephants endangered? (They are killed for their tusks and for their meat, and their habitat is being destroyed.)

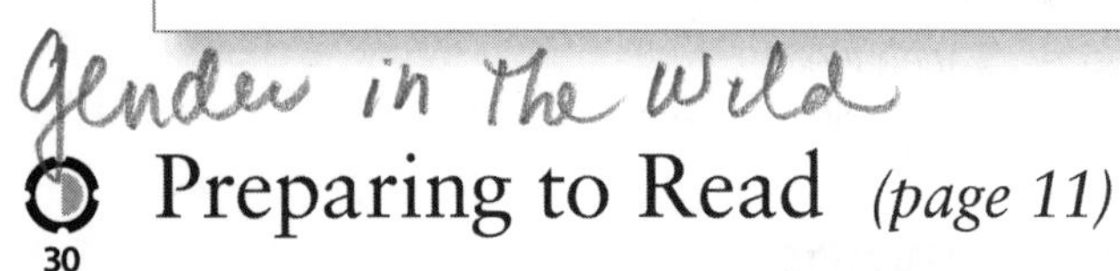

Preparing to Read *(page 11)*

30 mins

WARM-UP

Lesson B target vocabulary is presented in the context of gender and family relationships of animals in the wild.

Ask students to talk about which animals they like and why. Which ones do they think are most intelligent? Which ones are most like humans?

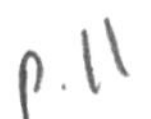

Exercise A. | Building Vocabulary

- Ask students to choose if they want to work individually or in pairs.
- Do the first item together with the class as an example.
- After checking the answer to item 9, draw students' attention to the **Word Link** box. Explain that learning prefixes like *pre-* can help to expand vocabulary. Ask if students can think of any other words using the prefix *pre-*. (See Ideas for Expansion, opposite.)

Answer Key

1. e **2.** c **3.** h **4.** f **5.** i **6.** j **7.** b **8.** d **9.** g **10.** a

IDEAS FOR . . . Expansion

For the **Word Link**, have a two-minute brainstorming activity where students work in small groups to think of as many words as possible that start with the prefix *pre-* meaning *before*. (Examples: *prehistoric, predate, preschool, preface*)

You may also want to add the prefix *post-* (meaning *after*) to this activity. (Examples: *postgraduate, postpone, postdate*)

Exercise B. | Using Vocabulary

- Remind students to respond to the questions with complete sentences.
- Students who finish early can make up additional questions using other words from exercise **A.**

Exercise C. | Predicting

Ask students what they can learn by looking at the photos and reading the captions, title, and the subheads. (This should tell them that the passage is about three different types of animals in three different countries.)

track 1-02

You may want students to listen to the audio as they read the passage. Explain that the vocabulary definitions in the footnotes at the bottom of pages 13 and 14 will help them understand the reading.

Overview of the Reading

The reading contains three articles about the influence of gender on family relationships in three different types of mammals: elephants, geladas, and chimpanzees. Each study shows that animals' roles differ according to whether they are male or female.

IDEAS FOR . . . Checking Comprehension

Ask these additional questions about the reading, or write them on the board.

1. Choose one behavioral characteristic described in the article and say how it is similar to or different from human behavior. (You may want to assign one characteristic to each group of students and ask them to discuss it in detail.)
2. What facts did you find most surprising in each of these three articles?

45 mins

Understanding the Reading *(pages 15–16)*

Check students' predictions in exercise **C** on page 11.

Answer Key

The correct answer is a. The idea that links all three stories together is the idea of gender roles in animal societies. Item b is not the correct answer because although the stories are based on scientific research in Africa, they are not all about primates (elephants are not primates). Item c is not the correct answer because only the second story is about a society with female power.

Exercise A. | Identifying Main Ideas

- Ask students to look back at the passage and try to identify the most important idea in each section.
- Discuss the main ideas briefly as a class and have students check their answers.

Answer Key

1. a **2.** b **3.** a

Exercise B. | Identifying Meaning from Context

- This exercise has three steps. First, students find and underline the words in the passage.
- Second, they figure out what the words mean from context. Do the first item as an example. (For example, as paragraph C is mainly about male elephants, the word *bull* probably means "male.")
- Third, they match the words with their definitions.
- Ask students to work in pairs to locate and discuss the meaning of the words.
- After everyone has had a chance to complete the exercise, check answers as a class, asking students to support their answers with reference to the original use of the word in the reading passage.

Answer Key

1. bull **2.** drought **3.** associations **4.** have little say **5.** in the wild **6.** mimicked

Exercise C. | Identifying Supporting Details

- Tell students to reread the passage and find the answers.
- Students who finish early can make up additional questions to ask the class.

Answer Key

1. They are killed by hunters or farmers. **2.** Older males control and discipline the younger males. **3.** One **4.** Because the male is not attentive enough to the females or their infants. **5.** Young female chimps **6.** Practicing for motherhood

Exercise D. | Critical Thinking: Evaluating Supporting Arguments

- Allow time for students to complete the sentences and discuss the answers in groups.
- Check the answers. Then discuss the final questions as a class. Ask if students can think of any alternative explanations for this behavior. What further research questions would they like to ask to verify these results?

Answer Key

1. study **2.** primatologist **3.** mimicked **4.** fourteen **5.** a hundred

Exercise E. | Critical Thinking: Synthesizing

- Encourage students to look back through the unit and reread previous passages.
- Check the answers by asking students to support their answers with reference to a specific part of the reading passage.

Answer Key

1. Geladas **2.** Elephants, geladas, chimpanzees **3.** Chimpanzees, elephants

45 mins

Exploring Written English

(pages 17–19)

- Read aloud the writing goal. Mention that comparison and contrast is one type of essay.
- Remind students that writing is a process. Just as there are stages of reading that lead to comprehension, there are stages in the writing process that lead to producing a final draft. The lesson starts with brainstorming, then goes on to a review of language for writing, and then presents the steps in the writing process.

Exercise A. | Brainstorming

- Remind students that brainstorming is a useful first step for gathering ideas before writing. They should choose two types of animal and come up with ideas to write about for each one.
- Go over the information in the box about **Free Writing.**
- Explain that *free writing* is writing rapidly in order to come up with ideas without worrying about mistakes.
- Make sure students understand each of the terms in the box.
- Set a time limit of five minutes for students to free write about their chosen animals.
- Note that these sentences will be used later in exercise **C** on page 18.

Exercise B.

- Go over the information and examples in the **Language for Writing** box.
- Write some easy examples on the board so that students can practice using these expressions—for example: *Female elephants take care of their young. Female chimpanzees feed and take care of their infants.*
- Point out the difference in punctuation when using the expressions at the beginning of a sentence or within a sentence.
- Allow time for students to write their answers.
- Monitor students as they work and pinpoint any trouble areas.
- Invite volunteers to write their answers on the board.

IDEAS FOR . . . Presenting Grammar

Point out that *while* is a subordinating conjunction and is used to join two clauses: a main clause and a subordinate clause. *Conversely* and *On the other hand* are transition phrases that show a link between sentences without joining them.

While can be used to introduce either the first or second clause of a sentence.

Contrast: Female elephants have strong bonds throughout their lives, *while* male elephants are more independent. / *While* male elephants are more independent, female elephants have strong bonds throughout their lives.

Write additional examples on the board of sentences without punctuation and ask students to come to the board and revise the sentence.

Answer Key

1. Social networking is important in the human workplace. In a similar way, chimpanzees form strong bonds within their groups.
2. Male geladas are big and have bushy manes, while female geladas are small and less distinctive looking. / While male geladas are big and have bushy manes, female geladas are small and less distinctive looking.
3. Young male chimps prefer active play. Conversely, young female chimps prefer less active play. / Young female chimps, conversely, prefer less active play.
4. Humans have invented tools to help them survive. Likewise, chimpanzees make and use tools for specific purposes.

Exercise C. | Applying

- Have students look back at their work in exercise **A** and rewrite their sentences.
- Monitor students as they work and offer help as needed.
- Ask volunteers to read sentences aloud or write them on the board.
- Provide feedback as required.

Writing Skill: Reviewing Paragraph Writing

- Go over the information in the box about paragraph writing.
- Check comprehension by asking: *What is a topic sentence? What are the supporting ideas? What is the purpose of details and examples?*

Exercise D. | Critical Thinking: Analyzing

- Use questions 1 and 2 in exercise **D** to analyze the topic sentence in the box.
- Tell students to work in pairs and analyze the paragraph.

Answer Key

1. Monkeys and apes
2. Differences and similarities (both)
3. Hand structures, intelligence / use of tools, cooperation / social groups
4. Apes have opposable thumbs, while monkeys do not. Chimpanzees, gorillas, and bonobos use tools, while only one species of monkey uses tools. Both apes and monkeys live in large family groups.

Writing Task: Drafting and Revising

(pages 20–21)

Exercise A. | Planning

- Point out that a Venn diagram is a useful way to organize ideas before writing.
- Draw a Venn diagram on the board, and model how to fill in the circles with one or two examples.
- Refer students back to the Writing Skill box on page 19 for an example of a good topic sentence.
- Ask students to read out their topic sentences, and ask for comments and feedback from the class.

Exercise B. | Draft 1

- Remind the class that the main purpose of a first draft is to get ideas down on paper.
- As students write their first draft, walk around and offer help as needed. It is not necessary to correct grammar at this stage.
- You may want to set this task for homework.

Exercise C. | Comparing

- Explain that most writing usually requires two or more drafts. Point out that in this activity, students will compare two drafts of a paragraph to see how revising can improve the first draft. Doing this activity will help students to revise their own writing.
- Students can work individually or in pairs to complete this task.
- Ask volunteers to explain the reasons for their choice.

Answer Key

Paragraph b is the first draft, and paragraph a is the revision.

Paragraph a has a good topic sentence at the beginning that identifies the three points of comparison. Paragraph b has a topic sentence at the end, and it is not very specific.

Paragraph b includes irrelevant information: *Some dogs make excellent pets, but some do not. The more intelligent a dog is, the better pet it can be.*

Paragraph b spends a lot of time on the second point of comparison and is repetitive.

Exercise D. | Critical Thinking: Analyzing

- Ask students to work in pairs to discuss their answers.
- Go over the answers together as a class.

Answer Key

	a	**b**
1.	Y	Y
2.	Y	Y
3.	Y	Y
4.	Y	N

Exercise E. | Revising

Remind students that it is important to learn how to reread their work carefully and look for ways to improve it.

Exercise F. | Peer Evaluation

- Explain that peer evaluation is a good way to get individualized feedback on your writing. All writers need to get feedback on their writing in order to improve.
- Discuss the three steps in the evaluation process to make sure students know what to do. (See page xiii of this book for ideas.)
- Ensure that both members of the pair have equal time to give feedback.

Writing Task: Editing

(page 22)

Exercise G. | Draft 2

Walk around and monitor students as they work. Provide assistance as needed.

Exercise H. | Editing Practice

- The purpose of this exercise is to give students additional practice in editing for grammar in preparation for using the Editing Checklist for their second draft.
- Go over the information in the box.
- Allow time for students to find and correct the mistakes.
- Invite volunteers to write the corrected sentences on the board.

Answer Key

1. The use of tools among gorillas **is** similar to the use of tools among chimpanzees.
2. Dogs are not capable of using language. Conversely, some apes are able to communicate using human sign language.
3. When greeting someone in Japan, it is the usual custom to bow. Likewise, people in Korea bow when they greet others.
4. In the U.K., people drive on the left side of the road. Drivers in the U.S.**,** on the other hand**,** drive on the right.
5. Chimpanzee mothers and daughters form strong bonds. In a similar way, adult female elephants form close relationships with young females in the family.

Exercise I. | Editing Checklist

- Read the sentences in the Editing Checklist.
- Allow time for students to read and edit their work.

Exercise J. | Final Draft

- Allow time for students to work on their final draft (or set this for homework).
- Collect their work.

TIP **You may want to suggest that students keep copies of their drafts in a portfolio so that they can see how their writing develops over the course of several drafts.**

IDEAS FOR . . . Further Research

Ask students to research another animal group not mentioned in this unit (for example, ants, bees, dolphins, penguins). What different types of social roles do they have and how are they similar to or different from human societies?

Science and Detection

Academic Track
History/Life Science

Academic Pathways:
Lesson A: Identifying a sequence of events
Distinguishing fact from speculation
Lesson B: Understanding a personal narrative/opinion article
Lesson C: Planning an opinion paragraph
Writing an opinion paragraph

Unit Theme

Unit 2 explores recent developments in technology that have helped experts to solve past mysteries.

Think and Discuss *(page 23)*

5 mins

- Ask students to describe the photo. Ask: *Who was Tutankhamun? How did they obtain his skull? How does the photo relate to the unit title?*
- Ask students to discuss the questions in groups.
- Write the groups' answers on the board.
- Note: Tutankhamun was a pharaoh of Ancient Egypt who ruled from 1332 BC to 1323 BC. More information about Tutankhamun can be found in the reading passage on pages 34–38 of this unit.

Answer Key

Possible answers:

1. X-rays and CT scans can help to locate missing objects; radiocarbon dating can identify the age of material; DNA can identify animals or people.
2. Examples: The ghost ship *Marie Celeste*, how the pyramids were built, the lost city of Atlantis

Exploring the Theme *(pages 24–25)*

15 mins

The opening spread features a scientist placing a skull in a CT scanner and includes information about three kinds of technology used in solving mysteries.

- Ask students to describe the main photo. Ask: *Who is he? What is he doing and why?*
- Ask students to read the information on the page.
- Have students work in groups to answer the questions.
- Call on volunteers to explain their answers to the class.
- Ask students to explain these additional terms from the text: *tumors, infections, internal bleeding, detectives, identifying markers, clay tablets, molecule, distinctive, victim.*

Vocabulary Notes

CT scan = computed tomography scan, i.e., X-rays that are processed by computer to create a 3D image
Note the difference between a CT scan and an MRI (magnetic resonance imaging) scan, which uses magnets and radio waves. CT scans are better at imaging bones, while MRI is better for soft structures such as the brain.
DNA = deoxyribonucleic acid, a molecule containing the unique genetic code for a living organism
Neanderthal = a human species that lived in Ice-Age Europe between about 200,000 and 28,000 years ago

Answer Key

1. CT scanners take 3D images of people or objects. They can be used for medical purposes or to solve mysteries.
2. Fingerprints were used in the second millennium BC to sign contracts and were first used to solve a crime in 1892.
3. DNA is useful for identifying people because everyone's DNA is unique. DNA is contained in every molecule of the body.

IDEAS FOR . . . Expansion

Ask students to find out more about nonmedical uses of CT scans, fingerprints, and DNA. Some examples are using CT scans to search for minerals underground, using fingerprints to provide secure access to computers or buildings, using DNA to trace the development of human evolution. Divide students into three groups and ask each group to choose one of these technologies to research. They can tell the class what they found out in the next lesson.

Tech Detectives

30 mins

Preparing to Read *(page 26)*

WARM-UP

The Lesson A target vocabulary is presented in the context of how modern technology has helped to solve crimes and mysteries.

Ask students to brainstorm how you might use the technologies mentioned on the previous page to solve a crime. What kind of evidence can be analyzed? What information might it provide?

Exercise A. | Building Vocabulary

- Have students find the words in the reading and use the other words around them to guess their meanings.
- As an example, do the first item together with the class.
- Check the answers by nominating one student to read out a word and a second student to read the matching definition. Continue around the class, nominating students at random.
- Ask students for other word forms of each word (for example, *identification, analyze, deduction).*
- Point out the **Word Link** box. Ask students to make sentences using these words.
- Tell students to use their dictionaries to find other words using the prefix *extra-*. (Possible answers: extradite, extrasensory, extramural)

Answer Key

1. attach
2. suspect
3. prime
4. commit [a crime]
5. detective
6. deduce
7. analysis
8. investigate
9. extract
10. identify

TIP **Review different ways to use context to find the meaning of the target vocabulary. For example, the opening sentence tells us that *detectives* are people who *solve crimes.***

Exercise B. | Using Vocabulary

- After students have discussed the questions with a partner, make a list of possible answers to each question on the board.
- For question 1, list the personal characteristics that would help someone investigate a crime.
- For question 2, list different types of evidence.
- For question 3, ask students to imagine that they are detectives trying to solve this case. What conclusions can they draw from the evidence?

Answer Key

Possible answers:
1. Patient, logical, persistent, determined
2. Fingerprints, DNA, eyewitness accounts, closed-circuit camera footage
3. The thief broke in through the front door and escaped through the kitchen window.

Exercise C. | Brainstorming

Invite a volunteer from each group to share their answers with the class.

Answer Key

Possible answers:
fingerprints, traces of material left at the scene of the crime, electronic trails, phone calls

Exercise D. | Predicting

- Encourage students to look at the title of the reading as well as the pictures and subheads. This will help them predict what the passage is about.
- There is no need to check the answers now. This will be done after students have finished reading the passage in detail.

track 1-03

You may want to play the audio while students read. Point out that the vocabulary definitions in the footnotes at the bottom of pages 27–28 will help them understand the reading.

Overview of the Reading

The passage describes some ways in which technology has been used to solve past mysteries. The technologies mentioned are DNA analysis and CT imaging. The mysteries relate to a robbery in Australia in 2009, a murder in Arizona in 1992, and a frozen mummy found in the Italian Alps in 1991.

More information about the discovery of the Iceman (nicknamed Ötzi because the body was found in the Ötz Valley) can be found at the website of the South Tyrol Archaeological Museum, http://www.iceman.it

Vocabulary Notes

Ask about or explain the meanings of these additional words in the reading.
leech (paragraph B) = small slug that attaches itself to animals and sucks their blood
speculate (paragraph B) = guess, draw conclusions that are not definite
unrelated (paragraph C) = not linked

arrest (paragraph C) = take into police custody
wrongdoing (paragraph D) = illegal behavior
collide (paragraph E) = crash
contradict (paragraph E) = say the opposite
arrowhead (paragraph G) = pointed tip of an arrow, made of stone or metal
wound (paragraph G) = injury
sustain (paragraph G) = receive, experience

IDEAS FOR . . . Checking Comprehension

Ask these additional questions about the reading, or write them on the board.

1. What do these three stories have in common? (All three situations used technology to solve a past crime.)
2. What is different about the last story? (This crime happened a very long time ago, and the body was preserved in the ice.)
3. In the first story, why were detectives not able to solve the crime at the time? (Because the men escaped.)
4. In the second story, what evidence did the police have and why was it not sufficient? (They found palo verde seed pods in the truck but could not prove they were from the tree at the scene of the crime.)
5. In the third story, what did the wounds on the Iceman's body tell the scientists? (That he had been in a fight some time previously, and that he was killed by an arrow.)
6. What is the significance of the Iceman's meal? (That he did not die of starvation, that he knew how to find food in the mountains, and that he had been settled in one place for at least a few hours before being killed.)
7. Which story do you find most unusual and interesting? Why?

IDEAS FOR . . . Expansion

Brainstorm a list of additional questions about the Iceman. Then ask students to find the answers by researching on the Internet. They can visit the website of the South Tyrol Archaeological Museum, where there is a lot of information about the find and the circumstances of the Iceman's death. http://www.iceman.it

Understanding the Reading

45 mins *(page 30)*

Check students' predictions in exercise **D** on page 26.

Answer Key

Plant DNA—a recent robbery (no, it was a murder)
Human DNA—a recent robbery (yes)
Human DNA—a recent murder (no, it was plant DNA)
Plant DNA—a recent murder (yes)
X-ray, CT scans—a preh... ...es)
X-ray, CT ... ...no, but the
mo... ...bery)

Exerc... ...deas

- First, ...ssage and try to ...
- Then a... ...ree rows in the cha...
- Draw th... chart on the board and check the answers by asking students to tell you which boxes to check.

Answer Key

	Leech Solves Robbery Case in Australia	Plant Helps Solve Murder Case in Arizona	Who Killed the Iceman?
1. X-rays			✓
2. CT imaging			✓
3. DNA	✓	✓	✓

Exercise B. | Identifying Key Details

- Allow time for students to complete the chart individually.
- Invite volunteers to come to the board to write their answers.
- Encourage others in the class to agree or disagree.

Answer Key

4. What evidence gave investigators useful information about the crime?	A leech filled with blood from the robber	DNA from the seed pods from a palo verde tree	An arrowhead in the Iceman's shoulder; a full stomach

Exercise C. | Critical Thinking: Distinguishing Fact from Speculation

- Read the information in the **CT Focus** box. Mention that distinguishing fact from speculation is an important tool in evaluating the arguments presented in a text.
- Allow time for students to complete their answers.
- Check the answers as a class.

TIP Before doing exercise C, you may want to read out some "facts" from the reading (for example: ***The leech attached itself to one of the robbers.***) and ask students to say whether it was fact or speculation. Then ask them to find the place in the text to check their answers.

Answer Key

1. S **2.** F (*proved, definitely*) **3.** S (*Perhaps, likely theory*) **4.** F (*clear*) **5.** S (*unlikely*)

Exercise D. | Speculating

Encourage students to use language from the **CT Focus** box in their discussions.

Answer Key

Possible answers:

Investigators think that he was having a meal in a safe place when he was attacked suddenly from behind, but it is also possible that he was sharing a meal with someone who then waited until he had moved some distance away before shooting him.

45 mins

Developing Reading Skills

(page 31)

Reading Skill: Identifying a Sequence of Events

- Ask students to retell the story of the Iceman, as far as they can remember it. While they are speaking, make note of any time expressions they use and write them on the board.
- Explain that these time expressions are important when telling or writing a story and also to understand the sequence of events in a reading passage.
- Go over the information in the box.
- Ask if students can think of any other time expressions.

Exercise A. | Analyzing

- After checking the answers, ask if students can add any other details to the story and where these details would go in the sequence.
- Draw a timeline on the board of events in the Iceman's story, and ask students to complete it in their notebooks.

Answer Key

2 Europe's oldest mummy, now known as the Iceman, was discovered by hikers in the frozen ice of the Italian Alps in 1991.

1 Scientists believe he lived about 5,300 years ago in an area north of what is now Bolzano, Italy.

3 New DNA analysis, along with X-ray and CT imaging technology, has helped scientists piece together even more clues about the life and death of this ancient Neolithic human.

Exercise B. | Applying

- To make this task more challenging, ask students to number the sentences first and then check their answers with the reading.
- Check the answers as a class.
- Ask students to identify any time expressions in the text.

Answer Key

a. 9 **b.** 6 **c.** 7 **d.** 2 **e.** 3 **f.** 1 **g.** 4 **h.** 5 **i.** 8

IDEAS FOR . . . Expansion

Ask students to create a timeline for the events in the second story. Draw the timeline on the board and ask volunteers to come up and write the events in the appropriate places.

30 mins

Viewing: Columbus DNA *(page 32)*

Overview of the Video

The video presents some information about attempts to identify the remains of Christopher Columbus and the controversy over where his remains are buried.

Vocabulary Notes

forensic = scientific methods used to solve crimes or mysteries
monarchy = royal family
fleet = group of ships
revere = respect, admire
remains = human bones
cede = give up
mausoleum = large building containing a tomb
unravel = solve
unearthed = discovered
degraded = deteriorated
enigma = mystery

Before Viewing

Exercise A. | Using a Dictionary

- Ask students to describe the photos. Ask what students know about Christopher Columbus. Why was he famous? What was controversial about him?
- Have students work in pairs to discuss the words and match them with their definitions.
- Compare answers as a class.

Answer Key

1. outcome **2.** conclusive **3.** contamination **4.** presumed **5.** controversy **6.** There's more to something than meets the eye

Exercise B. | Thinking Ahead

You may want to draw a chart on the board and ask students to complete it in their notebooks.

While Viewing

- Ask students to read the questions.
- Play the video while students write answers.

After Viewing

Exercise A.

- Have students work in pairs to discuss and compare answers.
- Play the video again and check answers.

Answer Key

1. Columbus wanted to be buried on Hispaniola.
2. The Spanish brought his remains back to Europe.
3. The Dominican Republic claims they brought the wrong bones back.
4. They're studying the bones of Columbus's relatives.

Exercise B. | Critical Thinking: Synthesizing

Remind students that *synthesizing* means relating different items of information and finding a common thread between them.

Answer Key

Scientific methods have enabled experts to analyze human remains or other evidence to identify who they belong to even many years later.

Note: The video mentions some controversy about Columbus's birthplace. Although most historians agree that Columbus was born in Genoa (now Italy), some speculate that he was born in Spain or Portugal.

IDEAS FOR . . . Checking Comprehension

Ask these additional questions about the video, or write them on the board.

1. How many ships did Columbus sail across the ocean with? (Three: the Pinta, Niña, and Santa Maria) When? (1492)
2. Why was the voyage important? (Before this, Europeans did not know about the Americas.)
3. Which countries are today located on the island of Hispaniola? (Haiti and the Dominican Republic)
4. Why is it difficult to work with 500-year-old bones? (They have deteriorated.)

King Tut

30 mins

Preparing to Read *(page 33)*

WARM-UP

Lesson B target vocabulary is presented in the context of research being carried out on the mummies and artifacts from the tombs of Egypt's ancient pharaohs.

Ask students what they think about doing research on mummies. Would they find it interesting, scary, weird?

Exercise A. | Building Vocabulary

- Ask students to choose if they want to work individually or in pairs.
- Explain that students should check the meaning in the passage first, before trying to answer the questions.
- After checking the answer to item 4, draw students' attention to the **Word Link** box. Ask students to explain the meanings of these words, using their dictionaries to help them.

Answer Key

1. sample	**6.** examination
2. scholar	**7.** identity
3. infectious	**8.** obtain
4. comprises	**9.** conduct
5. vulnerable	**10.** consequence

Exercise B. | Using Vocabulary

Remind students to use the target words in their answers if possible.

Answer Key

Possible answers:

1. arrest, prison **2.** weak immune system, chronic illness, age (infants or elderly) **3.** passport, ID card, fingerprints, DNA

Exercise C. | Brainstorming

- Remind students that brainstorming is a good way to predict what the passage will be about and will make it easier to understand.
- If students have trouble coming up with ideas, provide some question prompts: *Who were the Egyptian pharaohs? Why did they build pyramids? Why did they preserve their dead bodies as mummies? What was special about King Tutankhamun?*

Exercise D. | Predicting

- Ask students what they can learn by looking at the photos and reading the title and the subheads.
- Note: Students will check their predictions after reading in more detail.

track 1-04

Ask students to read the article. You may want to have them listen to the audio as they read. Explain that the vocabulary definitions in the footnotes on pages 35–38 will help them understand the reading.

Overview of the Reading

The reading contains an account of scientific analysis carried out on the mummified bodies of the ancient Egyptian pharaoh Tutankhamun and his relatives in order to establish his ancestry and the cause of his death.

Note: Some further vocabulary items from the reading passage will be studied in exercise **B** on page 39.

Vocabulary Notes

conflicting (paragraph A) = contradictory
partial (paragraph K) = incomplete
conceive (paragraph K) = create
erase (paragraph L) = delete

IDEAS FOR . . . Checking Comprehension

Ask these additional questions about the reading, or write them on the board.

1. What did you learn about Egyptian mummies and their burial rituals from this reading?
2. Using the information in the photos, what can you say about the art and culture of ancient Egypt?

45 mins

Understanding the Reading *(pages 39–40)*

Check students' predictions in exercise **D** on page 33.

Answer Key

The correct answers are b and c. The passage does not mention his political career.

Exercise A. | Identifying Main Ideas

- Do the first item as an example.
- Allow time for students to complete their answers individually.
- Compare answers as a class.
- As an extension, ask students to find the main idea of the remaining paragraphs: B, D, G, I, K, L

Answer Key

1. E **2.** J **3.**C **4.** H **5.** A **6.** F

Exercise B. | Identifying Meaning from Context

- This exercise has four steps. First, students find and underline the words in the passage.
- Second, they figure out the part of speech and what the words mean in context. Do the first item as an example. (For example, *honor* is a verb and probably means the same as *respect.*)
- Third, they write the part of speech and the definitions.
- Fourth, they check the meaning in a dictionary.
- Ask students to work in pairs to locate and discuss the meaning of the words.
- After everyone has had a chance to complete the exercise, check answers as a class. Discuss any differences between the meanings in context and the dictionary definitions.

Answer Key

1. honor (verb) = respect **2.** illustrate (verb) = explain, show **3.** tomb (noun) = burial place **4.** staffs (noun) = walking sticks **5.** mummification (noun) = process of making a mummy **6.** fracturing (verb) = breaking **7.** siblings (noun) = brothers or sisters

Exercise C. | Identifying Supporting Details

- Tell students to reread the passage and find the answers.
- Check the answers as a class and write them on the board.

Answer Key

1. Akhenaten and his sister
2. Ankhesenamun, his half sister
3. A genetic defect caused by members of the same family marrying each other
4. A club foot, bone disease, and malaria
5. King Tut was weakened by genetic defects.

Exercise D. | Identifying a Sequence of Events

- Allow time for students to complete their answers individually.
- Invite a student to come to the board and write the answers.
- Ask students to identify time expressions that helped them to identify sequence.

Answer Key

1. 6 **2.** 4 **3.** 3 **4.** 2 **5.** 1 **6.** 7 **7.** 5 **8.** 8

Exercise E. | Critical Thinking: Distinguishing Fact from Speculation

- Encourage students to look back through the unit and reread the relevant passages.
- As an extension, ask students to find further examples of facts or speculation from the passage. For example, *Some scholars had argued that the staffs were symbols of power.* (paragraph E, speculation)

Answer Key

1. F **2.** F (*show*) **3.** F (*discovery*) **4.** S (*Perhaps*) **5.** S (*opinion*) **6.** F (*proved*) **7.** S (*may have been*) **8.** S (*may, possibly*)

Exercise F. | Critical Thinking: Synthesizing

- Encourage students to look back through the unit and reread previous passages.
- Check the answers by asking students to support their answers with reference to a specific part of the reading passage.

Answer Key

Possible answers:

1. CT scans and DNA analysis
2. Both used CT scans to try and determine the cause of death. The Iceman investigation did not investigate his ancestry, and experts do not have as many clues in the form of historical records and artifacts as they do for Tutankhamun.

Exercise G. | Critical Thinking: Inferring Attitude

- Encourage students to look back at paragraph A to find the answers.
- Refer students to the final paragraph of the article to see how the author reconciles these two views.

Answer Key

Possible answers:

1. Because he feels we should respect the dead and not disturb them.
2. It is important to learn about history by examining them scientifically (and it helps to keep their memory alive).

45 mins

Exploring Written English
(pages 41–43)

- Read aloud the writing goal.
- Remind students of the steps in the writing process: analyzing the task, generating ideas (brainstorming and free writing), organizing ideas (planning), writing, revising, and editing.

Exercise A. | Brainstorming

- Remind students that brainstorming is a useful first step for gathering ideas before writing.
- Allow time for students to come up with ideas in pairs.
- Go over the information in the box about **Free Writing**.
- Remind students that *free writing* is writing rapidly in order to come up with ideas without worrying about mistakes.
- Set a time limit of five minutes for students to free write.

Exercise B.

- Go over the information and examples in the **Language for Writing** box.
- Ask students to make up one or two of their own examples using these verbs.
- Allow time for students to write their answers.
- Monitor students as they work and pinpoint any trouble spots.
- Invite volunteers to read out their answers.

IDEAS FOR . . . Presenting Grammar

The modal verb *should* is often used to give advice or to make a recommendation. It is a weak form of obligation.

The second example in the box is a hypothetical conditional sentence. The sentence is composed of two clauses. The main clause uses a modal such as *might, could,* or *would* together with a main verb. The subordinate clause (introduced by *if*) uses a verb in the simple past.

When the *if* clause comes first, there is a comma after the subordinate clause.

Answer Key

1. should **2.** should **3.** could/might **4.** could/might **5.** could/might **6.** could/might **7.** should **8.** could/might **9.** could/might

Exercise C. | Applying

- Allow time for students to write their sentences. Remind students to use modals.
- Ask volunteers to read out sentences or to write them on the board.
- Provide feedback on grammar as required.
- Lead into a broader discussion of this issue.

Writing Skill: Planning an Opinion Paragraph

- Go over the information in the box.
- Review page 19 in Unit 1 if necessary.

Exercise D. | Identifying Parts of an Opinion Paragraph

- Tell students to work in pairs to analyze the paragraph in exercise **B**.

Answer Key

The topic sentence is: I believe that people should not be required to give samples of their DNA in these situations.

The supporting ideas are: 1. A technician can make a mistake. (followed by an example) 2. A person may have been at the scene of a crime by chance.

P43

Exercise E. | Critical Thinking: Analyzing

- Read the directions and make sure students understand the terms *eyewitness* and *eyewitness account.*
- Ask for some suggestions as to whether eyewitness accounts are reliable or not and in what situations they might be unreliable.

Answer Key

a. T **b.** D **c.** S **d.** S **e.** D

Exercise F.

Make sure students know they should write a continuous paragraph (not separate sentences).

Answer Key

I do not believe that eyewitness accounts should be used in trials. One reason is that research shows we do not always remember things exactly the way they actually happened. For instance, our memory might change when we receive additional information about an event we experienced in the past. Another reason is that witnesses sometimes believe that if the police think a suspect committed a crime, that person must be guilty. Eyewitnesses might assume the police have other evidence against the suspect, and so they might believe they saw the suspect at the crime scene.

Writing Task: Drafting and Revising *(pages 44–45)*

Exercise A. | Planning

- Point out that an idea map is a useful way to organize ideas before writing.
- Draw the idea map on the board, and model how to fill in the circles with one or two examples.
- Allow time for students to complete their idea maps, using ideas from exercise **A** and **Free Writing** as appropriate.

Exercise B. | Draft 1

- Remind the class that the main purpose of a first draft is to get ideas down on paper.
- As students write their first draft, walk around and offer help as needed. It is not necessary to correct grammar at this stage.
- You may want to set this task for homework.

Exercise C. | Revising

- Explain that writing a paragraph usually requires two or more drafts. Point out that in this activity, students will compare two drafts of a paragraph to see how revising can improve the first draft. Doing this activity will help students to revise their own writing.
- Students can work individually or in pairs to complete this task.
- Ask volunteers to explain the reasons for their choice.

Answer Key

Item b is the first draft; item a is the revision.

Paragraph a has a strong topic sentence that clearly presents the writer's opinion. It has two main supporting arguments, and each argument is supported by details. Paragraph b has a topic sentence at the end, and it is not very specific.

Paragraph b includes irrelevant information: *Currently in many countries, people cannot be forced to provide a DNA sample, even if they are accused of a crime.* It also spends a lot of time on the first point but provides no support for the second point.

Exercise D. | Critical Thinking: Analyzing

- Ask students to work in pairs to discuss their answers.
- Go over the answers together as a class.

Answer Key

	a	b
1.	Y	Y
2.	Y	N
3.	Y	Y
4.	Y	N
5.	Y	Y

Exercise E. | Revising

Remind students that it is important to learn how to reread their work carefully and look for ways to improve it.

Exercise F. | Peer Evaluation

- Explain that this process will help students to see if they have organized their ideas clearly.
- Discuss the four steps in the evaluation process to make sure students know what to do. (See page xiii of this book for ideas.)
- Ensure that both members of the pair have equal time to give feedback.

Writing Task: Editing

(page 46)

Exercise G. | Draft 2

Walk around and monitor students as they work. Provide assistance as needed.

Exercise H. | Editing Practice

- The purpose of this exercise is to give students additional practice in editing for grammar in preparation for using the Editing Checklist for their second draft.
- Go over the information in the box.
- Allow time for students to find and correct the mistakes.
- Invite volunteers to write the corrected sentences on the board.

Answer Key

1. If governments had national DNA databanks, police could **find** criminals more easily.
2. In my opinion, no one **should** have to give DNA samples to the police.
3. Dishonest detectives might **use** DNA information in illegal ways.
4. I think researchers **should** continue to study the Iceman to learn more about the lives of people in prehistoric times.
5. Some researchers want to do CT scans of other pharaohs' mummies. It is possible the scans **could** prove how the pharaohs died.

Exercise I. | Editing Checklist

- Read aloud the sentences in the Editing Checklist.
- Allow time for students to read and edit their work.

Exercise J. | Final Draft

- Allow time for students to work on their final draft (or set this for homework).
- Collect their work.

IDEAS FOR . . . Further Research

Ask students to research another mystery from the past that technology has helped to solve. Some examples are: the ghost ship *Marie Celeste*, how the pyramids were built, the lost city of Atlantis, how the moai statues of Easter Island were built, why and how Stonehenge was built, the abandoned cities of Chaco Canyon.

Students may also be interested in following up a related story about how science was used to solve the murder of Pharaoh Rameses III, who ruled Egypt in the third century BC. More information can be found here:

http://www.livescience.com/25647-mummy-murder-mystery-solved.html

You may want to give each group a different mystery. They can present the results of their research in the next lesson or write about it in their journal.

City Solutions

Academic Track
Sociology

Academic Pathways:
Lesson A: Identifying reasons
Evaluating sources
Lesson B: Reading an interview
Lesson C: Writing a thesis statement
Writing descriptive paragraphs

Unit Theme

Unit 3 explores the causes and effects of urban population growth and the emergence of megacities around the world.

Think and Discuss *(page 47)*

5 mins

- Ask students to describe the photo. Ask: *What is it like to live in a city like this? What are the positives and the negatives? How does the unit title relate to the photo?*
- Ask students to discuss questions 1 and 2 in groups.
- Gather their answers as a class and write them on the board.

Exploring the Theme *(pages 48–49)*

15 mins

The opening spread features a photo of a crowded railway station in Mumbai, India, and three world maps showing the increase in the number of cities with more than a million inhabitants.

- Ask students to describe the main photo. Ask: *Why is it so crowded? What problems could there be? What does "the world's densest city" mean?* (The city with the highest number of inhabitants per square meter.)
- Discuss which cities students think are the largest in the world. (You may want to distinguish between cities that are large in area and those that are large in population.)
- Ask students to look at the third map to see if they were correct.
- Discuss what kind of information the maps show.
- Have students work in groups to answer the questions.
- Call on volunteers to explain their answers to the class.
- Brainstorm other possible reasons cities are growing. Ask students to give examples from their own countries or knowledge of other countries.

Answer Key

A.

1. 1900: London, 1950: New York, 2010: Tokyo
2. 36.7 million people
3. 1950–2010 (population of cities multiplied by five) Possible causes (answers will vary): migration in search of work and better opportunities.

B.

1. Asia, Africa, and Latin America
2. Large cities are overlapping to form huge cities. Populations are rising. People are migrating from rural areas.

IDEAS FOR . . . Expansion

Ask students to find out more about population growth. What kinds of changes are predicted? What are the main reasons for human population growth? What kinds of problems could it cause?

30 mins

Preparing to Read *(page 50)*

WARM-UP

The Lesson A target vocabulary is presented in the context of how urban populations around the world are growing.

Ask students whether they would prefer to live in a large city or in the country. What are the advantages and disadvantages of each?

Exercise A. | Building Vocabulary

- Have students find the words in the reading and use the other words around them to guess their meanings.
- Do the first item together with the class as an example.
- Allow time for students to complete their answers individually.
- As you check the answers, practice the pronunciation of these words if necessary.
- Point out the **Word Partners** box. Ask students to explain each of these phrases.

Answer Key

1. d **2.** f **3.** j **4.** g **5.** i **6.** h **7.** b **8.** e **9.** a **10.** c

TIP **Check the answers by writing the target words on the board. Then ask students to close their books. Finally, read out each definition and ask students to identify the target word.**

Exercise B. | Using Vocabulary

- For question 1, you may want to suggest some prompts such as work, family, education, sports, or creative, artistic, or spiritual activities.
- For question 2, list different types of problems on the board (for example, pollution, housing, overcrowding, crime).
- For question 3, ask students to predict changes in technology connected with, for example, communication, transportation, medicine, and housing.

Exercise C. | Brainstorming

- Divide students into two groups. Ask one group to brainstorm advantages, and the other group to brainstorm disadvantages.
- Draw a chart on the board with two columns. Ask a volunteer from each group to come to the board and write their ideas.

Answer Key

Possible answers:

Advantages: better facilities, better jobs, schools, hospitals, better standard of living, more entertainment

Disadvantages: noise, pollution, overcrowding, higher cost of living, expensive housing, smaller living spaces, more crime

Exercise D. | Predicting

- You may want to set a time limit of two minutes for students to predict what the passage is about.
- There is no need to check the answers now. This will be done after students have finished reading the passage in detail.

track **1-05**

You may want to play the audio while students read. Point out the vocabulary definitions in the footnotes at the bottom of pages 51 and 53.

Overview of the Reading

The passage describes some of the advantages of large cities, as well as some of the problems and suggested ways of tackling these problems through urban planning.

Vocabulary Notes

Ask about or explain the meanings of these additional words in the reading.
trend (paragraph A) = tendency
slum (paragraph B) = poorly built and often unhealthy housing in urban areas
flock (paragraph C) = move in a crowd
flow (paragraph C) = movement
ecological (paragraph D) = related to the study of the impact of humans on the environment
absorb (paragraph F) = take in
life expectancy (paragraph G) = length of life that people can expect to have

2/24

IDEAS FOR . . . Checking Comprehension

Ask these additional questions about the reading, or write them on the board.

A 1. Why does the author write that "humans have become an urban species"? (More than one-half of the people on Earth live in cities and that number is increasing.)
B 2. How have attitudes to big cities changed, and why have they changed? (Urbanization is now good news because many planners believe big cities offer a solution to the Earth's growing population.)
C 3. Why does the author compare the New York Stock Exchange with life in a modern city? (They work in one open, crowded space sharing information.)
G 4. How has life improved for South Koreans? Why do you think their life expectancy has increased? (As Seoul grew, so did the economy. Life has gotten much easier.)
5. Would you prefer to live in a suburb some miles away from your job, or in the center of a densely populated but well-designed city? (Answers will vary.)
6. Discuss the graphic on page 52. What does it show about the relationship between gas emissions and city density? (Large, dense cities emit less greenhouse gases.)

IDEAS FOR . . . Expansion Debate

Ask students to take notes on the advantages and disadvantages of large cities mentioned in the reading. Then divide the class into two groups. One group will be in favor of the growth of large cities. The other will be against. Allow some time for them to prepare their arguments. Then conduct a class debate on this topic.

45 mins

Understanding the Reading

(pages 54–55)

Check students' predictions in exercise **D** on page 50.

Answer Key

I think the reading is about the positive/negative aspects of living in cities and ways to manage population growth in cities in the future.

Exercise A. | Identifying Main Ideas

- Ask students to look back at the passage and identify the main idea of each paragraph.
- Call on volunteers to tell the class their answers and explain the reasons for their choices. Ask: *Which sentence in the paragraph provides the clue to the main idea?*
- As a follow-up, ask students to identify the main idea in the other paragraphs: F, H, I, J.

Answer Key

1. a **2.** a **3.** b **4.** a **5.** b **6.** b **7.** b

Exercise B. | Identifying Key Details

- Allow time for students to write their answers individually.
- Invite volunteers to read out their answers. Encourage others in the class to agree or disagree.

Answer Key

1. Two-thirds **2.** They were crowded, dirty, and unhealthy. **3.** It is cheaper to transport people, ideas, and goods. Cities attract and reward people with higher wages. **4.** They allow more people to live in less space and they have less of an impact on the environment. **5.** Economic growth paid for buildings, roads, and other infrastructure. **6.** Cities that are spreading out into surrounding areas **7.** Rising income and cheaper transportation **8.** Reducing the need to use cars and improving public transportation

Exercise C. | Critical Thinking: Evaluating Sources

- Read the information in the **CT Focus** box. Discuss the difference between a quote and a paraphrase. Mention why it is important to cite sources. (To make an argument more convincing and objective by giving it independent authority from an expert source, and to avoid plagiarism)
- Allow time for students to complete their answers.
- Check the answers as a class.

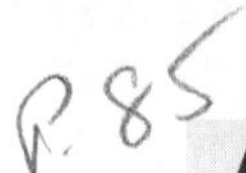

Answer Key

1. Paragraph C. This is a direct quote. It supports the importance of exchanging ideas quickly. Glaeser is a Harvard economist. It is an example of how people can tolerate smaller spaces if there are other advantages.
2. Paragraph D. This is a paraphrase. It supports the idea that large cities are good for the environment. Stewart Brand is an environmentalist (but we do not know what his credentials are). It strengthens the idea that large cities have many benefits.
3. Paragraph I. This is a direct quote. It explains one reason for urban sprawl. Shlomo Angel is an urban planning professor at New York University and Princeton University. It supports the argument that denser cities are more advantageous than spread-out cities.
4. Paragraph K. This is a paraphrase. It supports the idea that planning can help to create good cities. Shlomo Angel is an urban planning professor at New York University and Princeton University. It supports the argument that urban planning is essential to manage urban population growth.

Exercise D. | Personalizing

Encourage students to use ideas from the previous exercises and from the reading passage. You may want to set this exercise as a journal task for homework.

TIP **You may want to use this opportunity to remind students of the importance of academic honesty and how plagiarism is viewed by professors at U.S. and U.K. colleges. Perhaps your school or college has an academic honesty policy which it may be helpful to review at this point.**

45 mins

Developing Reading Skills

(page 56)

Reading Skill: Identifying Reasons

- Ask students to look back at paragraph C in the reading and identify any sentences that give the reasons cities are beneficial. (*Cities are productive because of "the absence of space between people," which reduces the cost of transporting goods, people, and ideas. . . . Successful cities attract and reward smart people with higher wages, and they enable people to learn from one another.)*
- Ask what question these sentences answer. (*Why/How are cities beneficial?)*
- Go over the information in the **Reading Skill** box.

Exercise A. | Understanding Reasons

- Explain that *identifying reasons* means understanding the relationship to different parts of the paragraph. Reasons are sometimes—but not always—indicated by the word *because*.
- Ask students to complete their answers individually.

Answer Key

1. People tend to rely more on cars to get to school and work or to go shopping.
2. Because the places where they work, shop, and relax are close together, residents can use low-energy forms of transportation, such as walking, biking, and public transportation, to get around.

Exercise B. | Applying

- Remind students to read the questions carefully and make sure their answers match the questions.
- Check the answers as a class.
- Finally, ask students if they can think of any counterarguments to the main premise of the reading passage.

Answer Key

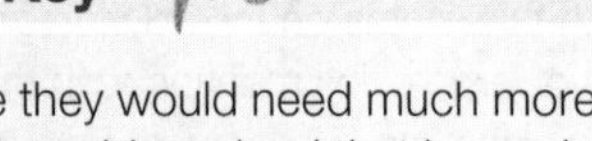

1. Because they would need much more space to live and they would use land that is needed for growing food.
2. Roads, sewers, and power lines are shorter. People living in cities use less energy to heat, cool, and light their homes.
3. Because people can walk or use public transportation.

IDEAS FOR . . . Expansion

Ask students to work in groups to create a design for their perfect city. Have them use some of the ideas in this lesson to label their design with the benefits of each design feature.

30 mins

Viewing: Solar Solutions *(page 57)*

Overview of the Video

The video presents some information about a project to introduce homemade solar-powered water heaters into homes in Cairo as a way to cut down on energy costs and improve the quality of life.

Vocabulary Notes

livestock = farm animals, such as chickens, sheep, and cattle
homeowner = person who owns a home
abundant = plentiful
circulate = move around
exotic = strange, unusual
innovation = new idea

Before Viewing

Exercise A. | Using a Dictionary

- Ask students to describe the photo and say what is unusual about the rooftops.
- Point out the location of Cairo on a world map. Ask what students know about Cairo.
- Have students work in pairs to discuss the words and match them with their definitions.
- Write the answers on the board.

Answer Key

1. cut down on **2.** going green **3.** a no-brainer **4.** found materials **5.** dwellers

Exercise B. | Thinking Ahead

- Discuss how solar panels work and what they can be used for.
- Ask if any students have solar panels in their homes and know how they work.
- After students have discussed the questions in pairs, compare answers as a class.
- Write students' ideas on the board without evaluating them.

While Viewing

- Ask students to read the questions.
- Play the video while students write answers to the questions.

Answer Key

1. He uses local community materials, recycled materials, and even some garbage.
2. Because they have abundant sunshine.
3. They're cheap to make, they improve the quality of life and sanitation, and they cut down on potential energy costs.
4. There's a lot of dust, and if you don't clean the solar heater, it doesn't work.
5. If you have a use for something, it is very valuable to you.

After Viewing

Exercise A.

- Have students work in pairs to discuss and compare answers.
- Play the video again if necessary and check the answers.

Exercise B. | Critical Thinking: Synthesizing

Remind students that *synthesizing* means relating information from different sources and finding connections between them.

Answer Key

Possible answer:

The solar water heaters would cut down on gas emissions, which would reduce pollution, and they would improve the quality of life for urban dwellers.

Quiz

IDEAS FOR . . . Checking Comprehension

Ask these additional questions about the video, or write them on the board.

1. What image of Cairo do most people have? (It is a big, busy city)
2. What kinds of things do Egyptians store on their rooftops? (Water tanks, satellite dishes, and livestock)
3. Why do they keep some of their garbage on their rooftops? (Because it may be useful one day)
4. Explain the following: *Cairo has been "going green" long before it became fashionable.* (People in Cairo are not in the habit of throwing things away, even when they are broken. They reuse things whenever possible, so they are environmentally responsible.)
5. How do the solar-powered heaters work? (They heat up water that circulates through metal tubes, eventually filling a tank with extremely hot water.)
6. What is especially interesting about this project? (It uses recycled materials and benefits the environment.)

30 mins

Preparing to Read *(page 58)*

WARM-UP

Lesson B target vocabulary is presented in the context of a study of data collected from major cities around the world.

Ask students how they think cities today are different from ten or twenty years ago. Are they better or worse?

Exercise A. | Building Vocabulary

- Ask students to choose if they want to work individually or in pairs.
- Explain that students should check the meaning in the passage first, before trying to match the words and the definitions.
- Ask students for other word forms of these words (for example, *sustainable, sustainability, justification, consumer).*
- Draw students' attention to the **Word Partners** box. Ask students to explain the meanings of these phrases and to make up other sentences using them.

Answer Key

1. sustain	**6.** objective
2. phenomenon	**7.** enhance
3. justified	**8.** statistical
4. majority	**9.** consistent
5. consumption	**10.** fundamental

Exercise B. | Using Vocabulary

- Remind students to use the target words in their answers if possible.
- Questions 4 and 5 can be used as the starting point for a more general discussion or for a journal entry.

Exercise C. | Predicting

- Ask students what they can learn by looking at the photos, the first paragraph, and the interview questions.
- Note: Students will check their predictions after reading in more detail.

track **1-06**

You may want to play the audio as students read the passage. Point out that the footnotes at the bottom of pages 59–61 will help students understand the reading.

Overview of the Reading

The reading contains an interview with Richard Wurman about a research project he has undertaken to collect information from major cities around the world in order to gain a better understanding of the urbanization process.

Note: Some additional vocabulary items will be studied in exercise **B** on page 62.

IDEAS FOR . . . Checking Comprehension

Ask these additional questions about the reading, or write them on the board.

1. What is Richard Wurman hoping to do with data he collects? (Use it to enhance the quality of life for people in cities while reducing the environmental impact of urbanization.)
2. Why was the existing data not very useful? (Much of the statistical information is gathered independently by city, and the questions asked are not always the same.)
3. What does he find fascinating about cities? (The world's largest cities change over time.)
4. What mistakes did urban planners make 30 years ago? (They tore down the slums and older parts of cities, and had urban renewal.)
5. What is bling architecture? Why does he dislike it? (It's the "showbiz part of architecture." He dislikes it because it has nothing to do with the fabric of the city.)
6. Why does he admire the city of Venice? (Because Venice's Piazza San Marco was made by the fabric of all the buildings around it.)

45 mins

Understanding the Reading *(pages 62–63)*

Check students' predictions in exercise **C** on page 58.

Answer Key

The correct answers are: **1.** a study on urbanization **2.** why people live in cities **3.** facts about some of the cities in the study **5.** urban architecture (The interview does not include information about **4.** the history of the modern city.)

Exercise A. | Identifying Main Ideas

- Refer students back to the passage to reread the relevant paragraphs.
- Allow time for students to complete their answers individually.
- Ask students to explain the reasons for their choices.
- As an extension, ask students to find the main idea of each of the remaining paragraphs: G, H, and J.

Answer Key

1. a **2.** b **3.** a **4.** a

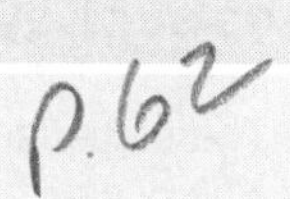

Exercise B. | Identifying Meaning from Context

- This exercise has four steps. First, students find and underline the words in the passage.
- Second, they figure out what the words mean in context.
- Third, they complete the definitions.
- Fourth, they check the meaning in a dictionary.
- Ask students to work in pairs to locate and discuss the meaning of the words.
- After everyone has had a chance to complete the exercise, check answers as a class.
- Discuss any differences between the meanings in context and the dictionary definitions.
- You may also want to comment on the figurative meaning of *flock* (literally, a group of sheep, goats, or birds) and *knit* (literally, to weave wool together).

Answer Key

1. gather **2.** comparison **3.** obvious **4.** poor
5. weaving, connecting **6.** go there **7.** accept

Exercise C. | Identifying Supporting Details

- Tell students to reread paragraphs D–F and underline relevant parts of the text.
- Discuss the answers as a class.

Answer Key

1. 19 cities that will have more than 20 million people in the 21st century
2. Extreme cities: Cities that are the largest, the oldest, the fastest growing, the lowest, the highest, the densest, the least dense, or the largest in area.

Exercise D. | Identifying Reasons

- Remind students of the skill of identifying reasons (page 56).
- Tell students to reread the relevant paragraphs and write their answers individually.
- After students have compared answers, ask volunteers to explain their answers to the class.

Answer Key

1. It helped to knit parts of the city together and reminds people that they're on the water (because they can see the Hudson River).
2. Because the buildings don't necessarily benefit the fabric of the city as a whole.
3. Because it attracts people from around the world and that brings about other improvements to the city.

Exercise E. | Critical Thinking: Evaluating Sources

- Ask students to work in groups. First, they should identify what each type of expert does. They can look back at the previous two readings to help them.
- Have students list at least three questions to ask each person.
- As an extension, you may ask students to role-play each of these roles in their group and describe what they could do for the city. The group can then take a vote on the three most convincing proposals.

Exercise F. | Critical Thinking: Synthesizing

- Encourage students to look back through the unit and reread previous passages.
- It may be helpful to have groups think of one sentence that embodies the main philosophy of each person.

Exercise G. | Personalizing

- It may be helpful to bring in some photos of famous buildings to help students in their discussions.
- Discuss any recent building development projects in your town or city, and ask whether students think any of them will improve the city and how.

IDEAS FOR . . . Expansion

Ask students to research the two urban projects mentioned in this reading passage: the High Line Park in Manhattan and the Guggenheim Museum in Bilbao. What was controversial about them? What effects did they have on the two cities?

Ask students to choose a famous "signature" building from cities around the world and research it for the next lesson. They can bring in a picture and a description and explain what was controversial about it and what effects it had on the city.

Some examples:
–The Shard, a 95-storey skyscraper in London, UK
–The Burj Al Arab (Tower of the Arabs) in Dubai, UAE
–The National Centre for the Performing Arts in Beijing, China
–The Sydney Opera House in Sydney, Australia

45 mins

Exploring Written English *(pages 64–65)*

- Read aloud the writing goal.
- Mention that a descriptive paragraph is different from an opinion paragraph (Unit 2) and a comparison paragraph (Unit 1).
- Ask students to tell you the steps in the writing process: analyzing the task, generating ideas (brainstorming and free writing), organizing ideas (planning), writing, revising, and editing.

Exercise A. | Brainstorming

- Give some examples of improvements in your city or a city that you know well. For example, there is a new cultural center; also, a large hospital that has more services has just opened downtown.
- Allow time for students to work in pairs to come up with ideas.
- Go over the information in the box about **Free Writing**.
- Set a time limit of five minutes for students to free write.

Exercise B.

- Go over the information and examples in the **Language for Writing** box.
- Review irregular past verb forms if necessary.
- Allow time for students to write their answers.
- Monitor students as they work and pinpoint any trouble spots.
- Invite volunteers to read their answers aloud.

IDEAS FOR . . . Presenting Grammar

Explain that *used to* describes states or actions that existed or happened regularly in the past, but do not exist or take place now.

To illustrate this concept, draw a chart on the board with two columns. In the left-hand column, write three things you used to do and three that you didn't use to do. In the right-hand column, write three things you do now and three things that you don't do now. Point out that there is no *d* at the end of *use* in the negative form.

Example:

past	now
play tennis every day	go swimming
(not) be a vegetarian	(not) eat meat

Ask students to make sentences about you using *used to*. Then ask them to make a similar chart about themselves and ask a partner to make sentences about them.

Answer Key

1. There used to be a lot of air pollution.
2. The buses ran on gasoline.
3. We didn't have a sports team in my city.
4. Downtown used to look very unattractive.

Exercise C. | Applying

- Allow time for students to write their sentences, referring back to their free writing from exercise **A**.
- Ask volunteers to read sentences aloud or to write them on the board.
- Provide feedback on grammar as required.

Writing Skill: Writing a Thesis Statement

- Go over the information in the box.
- Explain that a thesis statement encapsulates the main ideas of the essay and prepares the reader for the arguments that are to follow.
- Ask some comprehension questions about the information: *What is a body paragraph? What is the difference between a thesis statement and a topic statement?*

Exercise D. | Critical Thinking: Analyzing

- Go over the four characteristics of a thesis statement presented in the box.
- After students have discussed in pairs, compare answers as a class and discuss which statement in each pair is better and why.

TIP For exercise D, tell students to ask four questions about each pair of statements: *Does it present your position or opinion on the topic? Does it include the reasons for your opinion or position? Does it express only ideas that you can easily explain in the body paragraphs? Does it include key words that connect with the topic sentences of the body paragraphs?*

Answer Key

1. b **2.** a

Exercise E. | Applying

- Students may want to look back at their previous work in Units 1 and 2 to get ideas for this exercise.
- Monitor students as they work. Check that their reasons support their opinion. Tell them to check that their thesis statements meet the criteria in the box. (See **Tip** above. Tell students to ask these questions about their own thesis statements.)

Writing Task: Drafting and Revising *(pages 66–67)*

Exercise A. | Planning

- Point out that this planning chart is a useful way to organize ideas before writing.
- Go over the five steps in this exercise.
- Allow time for students to complete their charts, using ideas from exercise **A** and **Free Writing** as appropriate.
- Move around the class while students are writing, offering help and advice as needed.

Exercise B. | Draft 1

- Allow time for students to work individually.
- As students write their first draft, walk around and offer help as needed. It is not necessary to correct grammar at this stage.
- You may want to set this task for homework.

Exercise C. | Critical Thinking: Analyzing

- Explain that analyzing this model essay will help students to revise their own writing.
- Allow time for students to work in pairs.
- Identify any troublesome areas to focus on as a class.

Answer Key

1. **Thesis statement:** However, two recent changes have made the city an even better place to live—underground electrical wires and new bike lanes.
2. **Two reasons:** underground electrical wires and new bike lanes
3. **Topic sentences:** 1) Putting electrical wires underground is one thing that has improved the appearance of San Francisco. 2) Creating new bike lanes has also improved the quality of life in San Francisco.
4. **Key words in topic sentences:** underground electrical wires, new bike lanes
5. **Past:** In the past, the city used to have above-ground electrical wires hanging across every street. The wires hung on tall wooden poles that were placed on every block. The poles and the wires were unattractive. For example, in one neighborhood, North Beach, they blocked people's view of the sky, the trees, and the beautiful Victorian apartment buildings that lined the streets.
   Changes: Then, a few years ago, the city put all the electrical wires underground. This made the streets look much better. Today, people can enjoy the beautiful views as they walk down the streets in most San Francisco neighborhoods.
6. **Past:** It used to be dangerous to ride a bike in some areas of the city. Because they had to share the same lanes, cars and bikes were competing for space, and drivers injured many cyclists.
   Changes: In 2010, the city created special biking lanes going into and out of the downtown areas. These lanes encouraged more people to ride bikes instead of driving their cars downtown. Bike riding reduces the number of cars, so there's less traffic downtown now. Fewer cars on the road mean fewer greenhouse gas emissions, so the air quality is better in the city, too.

Exercise D. | Revising

- Explain that these steps will help students to reread their work carefully and look for ways to improve it.
- Walk around and monitor students as they work. Provide assistance as needed.

Exercise E. | Peer Evaluation

- Quickly discuss the four steps in the evaluation process. The purpose of this is to see if the writer has managed to convey the ideas set out in his or her outline.
- Ensure that both members of the pair have equal time to give feedback.

Writing Task: Editing

(page 68)

Exercise F. | Draft 2

Walk around and monitor students as they work. Provide assistance as needed.

Exercise G. | Editing Practice

- The purpose of this exercise is to give students additional practice in editing for grammar in preparation for using the Editing Checklist for their second draft.
- Go over the information in the box.
- Allow time for students to find and correct the mistakes.
- Invite volunteers to write the corrected sentences on the board.

Answer Key

1. The Empire State Building used **to** need a lot of energy, but now it is more energy-efficient.
2. The creek in downtown Seoul used to **be** covered in cement, but the city restored it.
3. Bangkok used to **be** very noisy, but the cars and motorcycles are much quieter now.
4. No buses **ran** in the downtown area, and this caused a lot of traffic.

Exercise H. | Editing Checklist

- Read the sentences in the Editing Checklist.
- Allow time for students to read and edit their work.

Exercise I. | Final Draft

- Allow time for students to work on their final draft (or set this for homework).
- Collect their work.

IDEAS FOR . . . Further Research

Ask students to research urban problems in different parts of the world and find out how they are being improved. You may want to assign a different city to each group and ask them to work on it together (examples: Rio de Janeiro, Beijing, Mumbai, Venice, Mexico City, Tokyo).

Danger Zones

Academic Track
Earth Science

Academic Pathways:
Lesson A: Organizing your notes
Analyzing and evaluating evidence
Lesson B: Interpreting information in a multimodal text
Lesson C: Writing an introductory paragraph
Writing a set of paragraphs

Unit Theme

Unit 4 explores the theme of natural disasters such as earthquakes, volcanic eruptions, hurricanes, floods, and drought. It examines how they are caused, why they are becoming more frequent, and whether they can be predicted.

Think and Discuss *(page 69)*

5 mins

- Ask students to describe the photo. Ask: *What countries have volcanoes? What happens when a volcano erupts?*
- Read the unit title and ask how it relates to the photo.
- Ask students to discuss the questions in groups, then discuss their answers as a class.

Exploring the Theme *(pages 70–71)*

15 mins

- The opening spread features a world map showing the locations where different types of hazardous natural events regularly occur. It also shows photos of four examples of such events: an earthquake, a volcanic eruption, a cyclone, and a tsunami.
- Tell them to look at the key and say what kind of information the map shows. Ask: *What do the different colors mean?* (The intensity of earthquakes) *What do the small white squares mean?* (The most dangerous volcanoes)
- Discuss question A as a class. Then ask students to read the information ("World of Hazards").
- Tell students to discuss questions B1–3 in groups.
- Discuss the answers as a class and ask what students know about each of the other natural events shown on these pages.

Vocabulary Notes

cyclone = large storm system that causes coastal flooding
inundation = flooding
plate boundaries = the boundaries between large plates that form the Earth's crust
storm surge = water that is pushed toward the coast by strong winds, sometimes combining with the natural tide to form an extreme and sudden increase in water level that floods the coast

Note: The Mercalli Scale is a 12-point scale describing the intensity of an earthquake according to its observable effects, ranging from 1 (not felt) to 12 (total destruction). The Richter Scale is based on the total amount of energy released by the earthquake and ranges from 0 to 9.

Answer Key

A. The red areas on the map are those with the most severe earthquakes.
B1. Most earthquakes and volcanoes are along the boundaries of tectonic plates.
2. Cyclones occur over water in the tropics (areas around the Tropic of Cancer and the Tropic of Capricorn).
3. They are areas with dense human populations.

IDEAS FOR . . . Expansion

Ask students to find out more about different types of natural disasters. They can present the results in the next lesson or create a diagram or poster for display in the classroom.

Possible questions for students to research: What causes this event? Where does it mainly occur? What effects does it have? Is it becoming more common?

Possible topics: typhoons, wildfires, avalanches, droughts, monsoons. (Note that hurricanes will be studied in the video section of this unit.)

30 mins

Preparing to Read *(page 72)*

WARM-UP

The Lesson A target vocabulary is presented in the context of the increasing risk of natural disasters.

Ask students what kinds of disasters are common in their countries and what they can do to prepare for them. Alternatively, discuss any natural disaster that has been in the news recently and talk about what caused it and how it could have been less destructive.

Exercise A. | Building Vocabulary

- Have students find the nine words in blue in the reading and use the other words around them to guess their meanings.
- You may want to ask them to list the words in their notebooks and write a possible meaning next to each one. For example, the word *reliable* could mean "certain," "definite," "dependable," or "good."
- Allow time for students to complete the exercise individually.
- Check the answers by asking students to read sentences aloud.
- After checking item 7, point out the **Word Link** box. Ask students to make up sentences using these words.
- Ask for other word forms of these words (for example, *concentrate, injury, emphasize, rely on).*
- Ask some general comprehension questions about the passage: *Who is the author? What kind of place does he or she live in? What is the problem facing their community? What is their solution? How would you feel in this situation? Who do you agree with?*

Answer Key

1. concentration	**6.** approximately
2. prone to	**7.** convinced
3. injured	**8.** reluctant to
4. commission	**9.** reliable
5. emphatic	

TIP **Ask groups to make up sentences using the target words. Tell them to write the sentences on a piece of paper with a blank for each target word. Then have them exchange papers with another group and write their answers.**

Exercise B. | Using Vocabulary

- Remind students to use the target words in their discussion.
- Compare answers as a class.

Exercise C. | Brainstorming

- For question 1, it may be interesting for students to work in groups with students from other countries if possible.
- For question 2, have students make a list of countries with active volcanoes (using the map on pages 70–71 to help them). Ask what students know about life in these countries.

Exercise D. | Predicting

- Ask students to describe the photos. How do they relate to the title and subheads?
- You may want to set a time limit of two minutes for students to predict what the passage is about.
- There is no need to check the answers now. This will be done after students have finished reading the passage in detail.

track **1-07**

You may want to play the audio while students read. Point out that the vocabulary definitions in the footnotes at the bottom of pages 73–74 will help them understand the reading.

Overview of the Reading

The passage describes why natural disasters are increasing and why more people are being affected by them. It states that it is impossible to predict natural disasters, but it is possible to prepare for them in order to minimize damage. It also describes the specific case of an earthquake that some people thought might have been predicted.

Vocabulary Notes

Ask about or explain the meanings of these additional words in the reading.

eruption (paragraph B) = explosion of gas, ash, and lava from a volcano
severity (paragraph B) = intensity, degree of damage
inland (paragraph C) = away from the coast
fertile land (paragraph F) = land that is good for agriculture
scenic beauty (paragraph F) = beautiful landscape or scenery
flood-control barrier (paragraph G) = wall that protects land from flooding
upgrading (paragraph J) = improving
in the event of (paragraph J) = in case of
sentenced (paragraph J) = be given a punishment by a court judge
imprecise (paragraph J) = inaccurate, opposite of *precise*
appeal (paragraph J) = challenge
conviction (paragraph J) = decision by a court judge that you have done something wrong

IDEAS FOR . . . Checking Comprehension

Ask these additional questions about the reading, or write them on the board.

1. Which natural disasters are mentioned in the passage? (Earthquakes, volcanic eruptions, hurricanes, floods, drought, tsunamis)
2. Compare the effects of global warming in Australia and Bangladesh. How are they the same and how are they different? (Australia does not have enough water and Bangladesh has too much. Both are losing crops, animals, and food.)
3. What are three methods being introduced to protect populations from disaster? (Floating houses, flood-control barriers, and green rooftops)
4. What signs seemed to indicate an earthquake in L'Aquila? (An increase in radon gas and tremors)
5. Why did scientists not believe Giuliani's prediction? (Because he had warned twice before and nothing had happened)
6. What can cities and towns do to prepare for an earthquake? (Upgrade existing buildings, build stronger new buildings, and educate citizens)

IDEAS FOR . . . Expansion

Ask students to research a major natural disaster that has occurred recently and find out as much as they can about the warning signs, the causes, the effects, and any other information.

45 mins

Understanding the Reading

(page 76)

Check students' predictions in exercise **D** on page 72.

Answer Key

The correct answer is b. (Item a is not correct because the article does not tell us how to deal with the damage, and c is not correct because the article does not tell us how to predict natural disasters.)

Exercise A. | Identifying Main Ideas

- Ask students to read the sentences. Then have them look back at the passage and identify the correct paragraphs.
- As a follow-up, ask students to identify the main idea in the other paragraphs: A, C, D, H, I.

Answer Key

1. G **2.** J **3.** B **4.** F **5.** E

Exercise B. | Identifying Key Details: Scanning for Numbers

- Remind students that *scanning* means glancing rapidly through the text to pick out specific information (in this case, numbers) and then reading the words around the number to determine what it represents.
- Allow time for students to write their answers individually.
- Ask volunteers to write their answers on the board.

Answer Key

1. d **2.** g **3.** e **4.** b **5.** c **6.** a **7.** f

Exercise C. | Identifying Reasons

- Allow time for students to write their answers individually.
- Draw the chart on the board and ask volunteers to come up and write their answers.

Answer Key

High-risk Area	Why It's Dangerous	Why People Live There
Near the coast	Flooding, tsunamis, and hurricanes	More jobs created by trade and international commerce; scenic beauty and outdoor activities
Close to volcanoes	Eruptions and volcanic lava	Fertile land for farming
Near rivers	Flooding	Fertile land for farming; scenic beauty and outdoor activities

Exercise D. | Critical Thinking: Analyzing Evidence

- Read the information in the **CT Focus** box.
- Remind students of the information about quotes and paraphrases in Unit 3.
- Discuss what makes a piece of evidence convincing or not.
- Allow time for students to complete their answers.
- Check the answers as a class.
- Ask students to find other quotes or facts in the reading—for example, in paragraph E—and evaluate them.

Answer Key

Claim: The risk of natural disasters is increasing.

Fact: In the past 15 years, there has also been an increase in the number of hurricanes hitting the U.S. coast.

Quote: "We expect the number of strikes over the next five years to be about 30 percent higher than the long-term historical average," says Robert Muir-Wood of Risk Management Solutions, a company that advises insurance companies.

Claim: Earthquakes cannot be predicted.

Fact: After the L'Aquila disaster, the Italian government asked U.S. seismologist Thomas Jordan to lead an international commission to determine whether earthquakes were predictable. The commission's answer was an emphatic no.

Quote: "It would be fantastic and exciting if we were able to predict the time and place of damaging earthquakes," says Michael Blanpied, a member of the National Earthquake Prediction Evaluation Council, "but so far we've had no success with specific predictions."

TIP You may want to use this opportunity to remind students of the importance of providing a list of references and sources with their assignments. When doing research on the Internet, for example, it is important to keep a record of relevant websites used as sources and list them in the references section at the end of the assignment. In this way, readers can check the reliability of the evidence presented.

Developing Reading Skills

(page 77)

Reading Skill: Organizing Your Notes

- Ask students to tell you what systems they use for taking notes from a reading. Compare different styles used by different students (for example, underlining with different colors or highlighting).
- Discuss why note taking is important.
- Go over the information in the **Reading Skill** box.
- Make sure students understand the different types of graphic organizers, and draw them on the board if necessary.

Exercise A. | Categorizing Information

- Refer students back to paragraph G in the reading passage.
- Allow time for students to complete the concept map individually.
- To check the answers, draw the concept map on the board and ask students to tell you what information goes in each space.
- Ask students to suggest any other ways of organizing this same information.

Answer Key

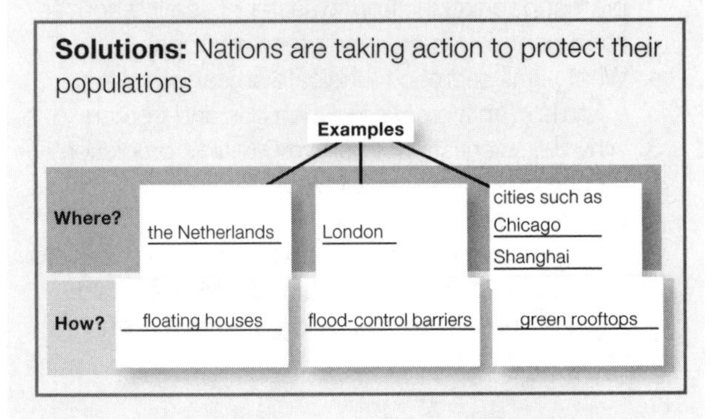

Exercise B. | Sequencing Information

- Refer students back to paragraphs H–J on page 74.
- Draw a timeline on the board. Write March 2009 in the center of the line. Then ask students to complete the timeline in their notebooks.
- Check the answers by asking students to tell you what to write and where to place it on the timeline.

Answer Key

Giuliani predicts earthquake twice → nothing happens → March 2009 → Giuliani predicts earthquake in L'Aquila → one week later → earthquake in L'Aquila → commission investigates if earthquakes are predictable → answer is no → October 2012 → six Italian scientists sentenced to prison for giving inaccurate information about earthquakes

IDEAS FOR . . . Expansion

Ask students to do some research about predicting earthquakes. What are some different possible ways of predicting them? Which ways have worked, and which ones have not worked? What methods of prediction are scientists working on at the moment?

30 mins

Viewing: Hurricanes *(page 78)*

Overview of the Video

The video presents some information about hurricanes: how they are formed, what kind of damage they cause, and how scientists try to predict their path.

Vocabulary Notes

driving rain = rain that is violent and forceful
killer waves = waves that cause death and destruction
spiral = ascend or descend in a circular motion
mainland = the continent, not the islands
vital = important
3-D = three-dimensional
awesome = amazing

Before Viewing

Exercise A. | Using a Dictionary

- Ask students to describe the photo and say what they know about hurricanes and tropical cyclones.
- Point out the location of Miami on a map. Ask what students know about Florida.
- Have students work individually to complete the task and then in pairs to compare answers.
- Write the answers on the board.

Answer Key

1. tropical **2.** warning **3.** atomic bomb **4.** sensor **5.** hallmark

Exercise B. | Thinking Ahead

- After students have completed the task individually, have them compare answers in pairs.
- Do not check answers yet as students will do this when they watch the video.

While Viewing

Play the video while students check the answers to exercise **B** and write answers to the questions.

After Viewing

Exercise A.

- Have students work in pairs to discuss and compare answers.
- Play the first part of the video again if necessary.
- Check the answers to exercise **B** and to **While Viewing** as a class.

Answer Key

Exercise B

5, 7, 2, 4, 1, 3, 6

While Viewing

1. "cyclone" or "typhoon"
2. As much as the explosion of half a million small atomic bombs
3. In the summer and fall

Exercise B. | Critical Thinking

- Remind students that connecting information from different sources will help them to remember and understand the information.
- Encourage students to find as many points of similarity and difference as possible.

Answer Key

Possible answers:

Both hurricanes and earthquakes are natural events that can cause extensive damage. Hurricanes are somewhat easier to predict.

IDEAS FOR . . . Checking Comprehension

Ask these additional questions about the video, or write them on the board.

1. How many hurricanes strike the mainland of North America in an average year? (Two or three)
2. What is a storm surge? (A wall of water that sweeps across the coastline where a hurricane makes landfall)
3. How many people were killed by hurricanes in the 20th century? (About 45,000 people)
4. How much damage did Hurricane Andrew cause? (25 billion dollars' worth of damage)
5. What are hurricane hunters? (Special planes that fly directly into the storms and drop sensors to measure wind speed, temperature, and air pressure, providing vital clues to the hurricane's direction)
6. What other methods are used to predict hurricanes? (3-D models)

yellowstone

Preparing to Read *(page 79)*

30 mins

WARM-UP

Lesson B target vocabulary is presented in the context of the volcanic formations in Yellowstone National Park.

Point out the location of Yellowstone National Park on a map of the U.S. Ask if any students have been there and what they know about the park. Why do people go there? What activities can they enjoy there? Ask students to look carefully at the photos on pages 80 and 82–83 and describe them.

Exercise A. | Building Vocabulary

- Ask students to choose if they want to work individually or in pairs.
- Explain that students should check the meaning in the passage first, before trying to match the words and the definitions.

Answer Key

1. d **2.** e **3.** h **4.** i **5.** b **6.** f **7.** c **8.** j **9.** a **10.** g

Exercise B. | Using Vocabulary

- Remind students to use the target words in their answers if possible.
- Draw students' attention to the **Word Partners** box. Ask students to make up sentences using these expressions.

Exercise C. | Brainstorming

- Ask students to work in groups. They can gather their ideas in a map or a chart.
- Write on the board any new vocabulary that comes up.

Exercise D. | Predicting

- Ask students to look at the photos and the captions as well as the title and the headings.
- Note: Students will check their predictions after reading in more detail.

track 1-08

You may want to play the audio while students read. Point out the footnote at the bottom of page 84; its purpose is to help students understand the reading.

Overview of the Reading

The reading describes the supervolcano that forms part of Yellowstone National Park and explains how the volcano was formed, how it was discovered, and whether it will erupt again.

Vocabulary Notes

extinction (paragraph A) = the state of being no longer in existence
intense (paragraph B) = extreme
plume (paragraph B) = a rising column of material such as gas, smoke, ash, or lava (See photo on page 81.)
chamber (paragraph B) = enclosed space
crater (paragraph B) = a bowl-shaped depression
theorize (paragraph C) = speculate
blast (infographic page 84) = explosion
plateau (infographic page 84) = a flat piece of land

Note: Some further vocabulary items will be studied in exercise **B** on page 85.

IDEAS FOR . . . Checking Comprehension

Ask students to look at paragraph D and tell you if these statements are true or false.

Which of these happened after the eruption of the supervolcano?

1. Light from the sun was reduced. (T)
2. A column of ash rose a million feet into the air. (F)
3. Winds carried the ash to California. (T)
4. Gas heated up to over 2,000 degrees Fahrenheit. (F)
5. The lava formed layers of rock that were over 100 feet thick. (T)

Ask students to choose another paragraph and make a set of five true-or-false statements to ask the class. You may want to assign a different paragraph to each group.

Understanding the Reading *(pages 85–86)*

45 mins

Check students' predictions in exercise D on page 79.

Answer Key

1. Explanatory text, infographics (pages 81 and 84), and timeline (page 82)
2. The correct answer is a (how a specific supervolcano in the USA was formed)

Exercise A. | Identifying Main Ideas

- Refer students back to the passage to reread the relevant paragraphs.
- Allow time for students to complete their answers individually.

Answer Key

1. difficult, eruption
2. rising, and falling land
3. No one, will

Exercise B. | Identifying Meaning from Context

- This exercise has four steps. First, students find and underline the words in the passage.
- Second, they figure out what the words mean in context.
- Third, they complete the definitions.
- Fourth, they check the meaning in a dictionary.
- Ask students to work in pairs to locate and discuss the meaning of the words.
- Check the answers as a class.
- Discuss other contexts in which these words could be used.

Answer Key

1. very large **2.** in the atmosphere **3.** destructive
4. after

Exercise C. | Identifying Key Details

- Tell students to locate the paragraphs that contain the answers to these questions. Then ask them to underline the relevant information.
- Discuss the answers as a class.

Answer Key

1. A supervolcano is bigger and more powerful.
2. Three times
3. The caldera was formed some 640,000 years ago after the last super-eruption
4. Scientists do not completely understand what happens under the surface. Records have only been kept since the 1970s.

Exercise D. | Understanding Infographics

- Ask students to explain what an infographic is. How does it help us to understand information?
- Discuss the infographic on page 84 and ask what kind of information it shows.
- Check the answers.

Answer Key

1. In the first eruption, 2.1 million years ago
2. 640,000 years ago

Exercise E. | Labeling a Process Diagram

- Point out that the three diagrams are shown in sequence from left to right.
- Ask students to locate the paragraph in the reading that contains this information (paragraph B).
- Ask students to work in pairs to label the diagram.
- As a review, ask students to describe the process to a partner by just looking at the diagram. Their partner can look at the description and help by giving prompts. Remind them to use sequence words such as *First, Next, Then, After that.*

Answer Key

Before the Eruption: b and f
The Volcano Erupts: e and d
After the Eruption: a and c

Exercise F. | Critical Thinking: Analyzing Evidence

- Remind students of the difference between fact and speculation.
- Tell students to underline the relevant parts of the text.

Answer Key

1. There is a huge open space surrounded by mountains. There is a thick layer of heated and compacted ash.
2. Land near the caldera has risen by 30 inches. A number of small earthquakes strike the area. The ground above the caldera is rising and falling.

Exercise G. | Critical Thinking: Synthesizing

Tell students to work in groups and come up with at least five similarities.

Answer Key

Possible answers:

They are natural events. They are unpredictable. They cause a lot of destruction. They are caused by a buildup of pressure under the Earth's surface.

IDEAS FOR . . . Expansion

Ask students to research another famous volcano and find out as much as they can about its formation and its history. They can present their information to the class using diagrams and infographics if possible.

Alternatively, have students find out as much as they can about the origins of the National Parks in the U.S. and when and why they were created.

45 mins

Exploring Written English

(pages 87–88)

- Refer back to page 41 in Unit 2, and remind students of the opinion paragraph they wrote previously and the use of modals of obligation and possibility.
- Read aloud the writing goal. Point out that the task asks for two types of recommendations: for individuals and for governments. Ask for some suggestions for how these could be different.

Exercise A. | Brainstorming

- Encourage students to look back through the unit to get ideas for the chart.
- Allow time for students to come up with ideas in pairs.
- Go over the information in the box about **Free Writing**.
- Set a time limit of five minutes for students to free write.

Exercise B.

- Explain the meaning of the words *parallel* (similar) and *structure* (grammar).
- Go over the information and examples in the **Language for Writing** box.
- Ask students to explain why the examples given are not parallel. (In the first one, for example, one sentence is active and the other is passive.)
- Allow time for students to complete their answers individually.
- Invite volunteers to read their answers aloud.

Answer Key

1. water, food
2. slippery, dangerous
3. cautious, aware
4. crushed, carried
5. frighten, damage

Writing Skill: Writing an Introductory Paragraph

- Go over the information in the box.
- Check comprehension by asking what the purpose of an introductory paragraph is. (To tell the reader what the essay will be about, and to grab the reader's interest)
- Look back at page 80 and read the introductory sentence. How does it grab the reader's interest?
- Look back at the opening paragraphs of other reading passages in the book and ask students to analyze them.

Exercise C. | Critical Thinking: Analyzing

After students have discussed in pairs, compare answers as a class and discuss which paragraph is better and why.

Answer Key

1. Thesis statement in paragraph A: *Fortunately, however, there are a few things you can do to make your house a safe place for you and your family.*

   Thesis statement in paragraph B: *In this essay, I'm going to provide some ways to protect yourself from home accidents.*
2. The essay is going to be about ways to make your home safe.
3. Paragraph A has a more engaging opening: *Most people may not realize it, but your home can be a very dangerous place.*
4. Paragraph A is better because:
   It has a more engaging opening.
   It avoids use of "I'm going to write about . . ." in the thesis statement.

Writing Task: Drafting

(page 89)

Exercise A. | Planning

- Point out that this planning chart is a useful way to organize ideas before writing.
- Go over the four steps in this exercise.
- Allow time for students to complete their charts, using ideas from exercise A and **Free Writing** as appropriate.
- Move around the class while students are writing, offering help and advice as needed.
- Ask one or two students to read their opening sentence aloud.

Exercise B. | Draft 1

- As students write their first draft, walk around and offer help as needed. It is not necessary to correct grammar at this stage.
- You may want to set this task for homework.

Writing Task: Revising

(pages 90–91)

Exercise C. | Critical Thinking: Analyzing

- Explain that analyzing this model essay will help students to revise their own writing.
- Allow time for students to work in pairs.
- Ask students for their opinions about what they liked or disliked in this essay.

Answer Key

1. **Opening statement:** When most people plan a vacation, they tend to spend a lot of time choosing a hotel, finding a good flight, and deciding what sites they want to see, but they may not plan for possible travel emergencies.
2. **Thesis statement:** In order to be prepared for an emergency, travelers should think about their medical needs, and also consider what they might need in case of the theft or loss of important items.
3. **Topic sentences:** 1) Thinking about their medical needs beforehand can save travelers a lot of time and trouble. 2) People should also consider what they might need in case of the theft or loss of items such as passports and credit cards.
4. **Key words in topic sentences:** medical needs, theft or loss
5. They should pack enough medication to last for the whole trip so they don't have to refill prescriptions while they're traveling. They should also keep their prescription medications in the original bottles, so that if they do have to refill a prescription for some reason, they will know the name of the medication and the dosage.
6. It's a good idea for travelers to know the phone numbers of their embassies or consulates in case their passports are stolen. Travelers should also leave copies of their passports with friends or family members at home, and they should also keep copies in different parts of their luggage. This way it will be easier to get replacement passports if necessary. Finally, people who are traveling should know the phone numbers of their credit card companies so they can cancel their cards immediately after they are lost or stolen.

Exercise D. | Revising

Explain that these steps will help students to reread their work carefully and look for ways to improve it.

Exercise E. | Peer Evaluation

- Explain that this process will help students to see if they have organized their ideas clearly.
- Discuss the four steps in the evaluation process to make sure students know what to do.
- Ensure that both members of the pair have equal time to give feedback.

Writing Task: Editing

(page 92)

Exercise F. | Draft 2

Walk around and monitor students as they work. Provide assistance as needed.

Exercise G. | Editing Practice

- The purpose of this exercise is to give students additional practice in editing for grammar in preparation for using the Editing Checklist for their second draft.
- Go over the information in the box.
- Allow time for students to find and correct the mistakes.
- Invite volunteers to write the corrected sentences on the board.

Answer Key

1. People can prepare for fires by creating an escape plan and **discussing** the plan with family members.
2. Keep important papers and **put** medicine in one place.
3. If you will need to take pets with you, pet carriers **and extra pet food are important to have.**
4. Walk around your house and **identify** things you will need to take.
5. Pack a bag with clothes **and necessities for each family member.**

Exercise H. | Editing Checklist

- Read the sentences in the Editing Checklist.
- Allow time for students to read and edit their work.

Exercise I. | Final Draft

- Allow time for students to work on their final draft (or set this for homework).
- Collect their work.

IDEAS FOR . . . Further Research

Ask students to research what to do in case of an emergency. Have them research government and other websites and tell the class about the most helpful websites. Have students work in groups to prepare a poster with essential information about what to do in case of a fire, a flood, an earthquake, a hurricane, etc.

UNIT

The Business of Tourism

5

Academic Track
Economics/Business

Academic Pathways:
Lesson A: Analyzing causes and effects
Analyzing a writer's argument
Lesson B: Reading related travel news reports
Lesson C: Writing well-developed body paragraphs
Writing a short cause-effect essay

Unit Theme

Unit 5 explores the theme of the possible negative effects of mass tourism and presents some solutions to managing tourism so that it does not damage the environment and also benefits the local community.

Think and Discuss *(page 93)*

5 mins

- Ask students to describe the photo. Ask: *What is the Taj Mahal? Why do people want to go there?*
- Brainstorm answers to these two questions with the class.
- Draw a chart with two columns on the board and write the benefits on one side and the problems on the other.

Exploring the Theme *(pages 94–95)*

15 mins

- The opening spread features a bar chart and a world map showing which countries are most popular with tourists, as well as a photo of tourists in the Louvre Museum in Paris, France.
- Ask students to describe the photo. Point out that the photo is taken from the point of view of the *Mona Lisa* painting, so the painting itself is not visible. Ask: *Why is the* Mona Lisa *so famous? Why do so many people want to see it?*
- Ask students to study the map and the chart. Ask: *What do the different colors mean in the chart and in the map?* (The number of tourists who visit each year.)
- Have students discuss questions 1–3 in groups. Then compare answers as a class.
- Ask students to come up with a list of factors that make a country popular with tourists, and write them on the board. Rank them in order of importance—for example, *historic buildings and ancient sites, climate, safety, cost, transportation.*

Answer Key

1. France

2. China and South Africa

3. Answers will vary.

Notes:
Taj Mahal = a white marble mausoleum in Agra, India, built in 1653 by the Mughal emperor Shah Jahan in memory of his dead wife. Over two million tourists visit it each year.

Mona Lisa = a portrait of a woman with an enigmatic smile, painted by the Italian artist Leonardo da Vinci. It is one of the most famous paintings in the world.

the Louvre = a museum in Paris containing thousands of historical objects, paintings, and sculptures. It has over 8 million visitors each year and is the world's most visited museum.

IDEAS FOR . . . Expansion

Ask students to choose one country and find out about tourism there. Why do people go there, and what do they do there? How is tourism affecting the country's economy? How is it affecting the country's heritage?

30 mins

Preparing to Read *(page 96)*

WARM-UP

The Lesson A target vocabulary is presented in the context of ecologically responsible tourism.

Ask students where they went for their last vacation. Take a class survey of the destinations, methods of travel, and types of accommodations. Ask students to explain why they chose their vacation.

Exercise A. | Building Vocabulary

- Have students find the words in blue in the reading and use the other words around them to guess their meanings.
- Allow time for students to complete the exercise individually.
- Check the answers by asking students to read sentences aloud.
- Point out the **Word Link** box. Ask students to explain the meaning of these words and to think of any other words using the root *mot*. (Possible answers: motion, motor)
- You may want to mention another meaning of *promote* (to be moved to a higher level of job).

Answer Key

1. enormous	**6.** core
2. alternative	**7.** advocate
3. promote	**8.** scope
4. via	**9.** distinctive
5. expand	**10.** partnership

Tell students to use their dictionaries to find other contexts in which these words are used and any other possible meanings and word partnerships.

Exercise B. | Using Vocabulary

- Remind students to use the target words in their discussion.
- Compare answers as a class.

Exercise C. | Brainstorming

- For question 1, it may be interesting to compare different types of tourism—group travel and backpackers, for example.
- For question 2, ask students to give examples of places they know that have been changed by tourism.
- For question 3, compare different resources available nowadays for learning about new places (for example, websites, interactive maps, GPS).

Exercise D. | Predicting

- Ask students to describe the photo. How might it relate to the title?
- Read the first paragraph aloud or play the audio.
- Ask students to define *mass tourism* (movements of large groups of tourists) and *tourism explosion* (sudden increase in tourism).
- Ask: *How might these tourist destinations be endangered? What kind of alternative could geotourism offer?*

track 1-09

You may want to play the audio while students read. Point out that the vocabulary definitions in the footnotes at the bottom of pages 97–99 will help them understand the reading.

Overview of the Reading

The passage describes some of the benefits of geotourism, a type of tourism that helps to sustain and enhance the geographical character and well-being of a place. It describes some of the negative effects of traditional tourism and explains why geotourism is a positive alternative.

Vocabulary Notes

Ask about or explain the meanings of these additional words in the reading.

pack ice (photo caption) = floating ice
explosion (paragraph A) = sudden increase
mission (paragraph B) = aim, goal
come up with (paragraph B) = invent
remote (paragraph B) = distant
sustain (paragraph D) = maintain and support
on a large scale (paragraph F) = widespread, extensively
petrified (paragraph G) = turned to stone
park ranger (paragraph G) = officer in charge of maintaining a park or forest
cuisine (paragraph H) = food, cooking

IDEAS FOR . . . Checking Comprehension

Ask these additional questions about the reading, or write them on the board.

1. Find five differences between geotourism and traditional tourism.
2. Describe one place that tourism has harmed and one place that it has helped.
3. What difficulties do you think there might be in persuading people to try geotourism? How would you persuade them?

IDEAS FOR . . . Expansion

Ask students to research endangered regions of the world and find out how tourism is benefiting or harming them. Examples: Monument Valley (shown in photo), the Grand Canyon, the Arctic, the Amazon Rainforest, Machu Picchu in Peru, the Cappadocian Caves in Turkey, the Galápagos Islands. (Note that the Galápagos Islands are the topic of the video in the next lesson.)

45 mins

Understanding the Reading

(page 100)

Check students' predictions in exercise **D** on page 96.

Answer Key

Geotourism is tourism that sustains or enhances the geographical character of a place.

Possible solutions: Geotourism can help money stay in local communities and can help tourists understand more of the nature and culture of the places they visit. It protects local people and environments.

Exercise A. | Identifying Main Ideas

- Ask students to read the sentences. Then have them look back at the passage and identify the correct paragraphs.
- As a follow-up, ask students to identify the main idea in the other paragraphs: D, G, I.

Answer Key

1. C **2.** H **3.** E **4.** J **5.** F **6.** B **7.** A

Exercise B. | Identifying Supporting Details

- Allow time for students to write their answers individually.
- Tell students to check their answers by looking back at the reading.
- Write the answers on the board.

Answer Key

1. A **2.** E **3.** J **4.** H **5.** C **6.** F

Exercise C. | Critical Thinking: Analyzing an Argument

- Read the information in the **CT Focus** box.
- Give an example to illustrate this point. For example (benefit): It's good to stay in locally owned hotels because they are more distinctive. (drawback of alternative): When you stay in large chain hotels, they are the same everywhere.
- Allow time for students to write their answers individually.
- Ask volunteers to write their answers on the board.
- As a review, ask students to close their books and try to remember the advantages of geotourism and the disadvantages of traditional tourism.
- Ask if students can think of any additional points to support geotourism.

Answer Key

Advantages of geotourism: a, c, f

Disadvantages of traditional tourism: b, d, e

Exercise D. | Critical Thinking: Evaluating an Argument

- Ask students to take the opposing view (in support of traditional tourism) and see how many arguments they can come up with.
- You may want to ask pairs of students to role-play a debate between two people with opposing points of view—for example, a tour company owner and a local restaurant owner.
- Have students make a list of tourist destinations in your area and evaluate how well each of them is managed. Do they benefit the local community? Do they protect the environment?

IDEAS FOR . . . Expansion

Ask students about vacations they have taken in the past. Where did they go? Where did they stay? What criteria did they use to choose their destination, method of travel, and accommodations? How well was the place managed? Did their vacation benefit the local community? Did it protect the environment?

Ask students to compare one vacation place that was managed well and one that was not. Have them tell the class about their experience or write about it in their journal.

45 mins

Developing Reading Skills *(page 101)*

Reading Skill: Analyzing Causes and Effects

- Write some easy examples of causes and effects on the board. For example: **Cause:** Many large hotels have been built on the coast. **Effect:** The beaches are crowded, and the water is polluted.
- Ask students to think of some other causes and effects related to the topic of tourism.
- Go over the information in the **Reading Skill** box.
- Study the example. What does the phrase *As a result* do? (It relates the second sentence to the first one and shows that one is the effect of the other.)
- Point out the difference between words that are conjunctions and join two clauses (*because, if, when, so*) and transition phrases that make a link between two separate sentences.
- Ask students if they know any other words or phrases that signal cause and effect—for example:

Cause: *due to, owing to, because of, since, one reason for, one reason why, one cause of*

Effect: *for this reason, as a consequence, this results in, one effect of, as a result of*

Exercise A. | Analyzing

- Allow time for students to read the paragraph and underline the signal words.
- You may want to ask students to draw a wavy line under causes and a dotted line under effects before completing the chart.
- To check the answers, draw the chart on the board and ask students to tell you what information goes in each space.
- Ask students to rephrase the causes and effects using other signal words from the **Reading Skill** box.

Answer Key

Signal words used in paragraph: *because, led to, Thus*

Cause	Effect
1. Ecotourism can bring significant economic benefits. **2.** The rise of ecotourism **3.** Local people often respond to the growing number of tourists by finding jobs as tour guides or starting small tourist-oriented businesses.	**1.** Many local and national governments are looking at ways to preserve their distinctive natural areas. **2.** The creation of several national parks and reserves where wildlife is protected **3.** Local people can increase their income and improve their standard of living.

Exercise B. | Applying

- Refer students back to paragraphs F and H on page 98.
- Point out that students should read the whole paragraphs to understand the main ideas.
- Check the answers and ask if they can add any other effects to this chart.

Answer Key

	Cause	Effect
F	badly managed tourism	Coasts and mountains can be destroyed.
H	well-managed tourism	Geographical diversity and distinctiveness can be preserved.

IDEAS FOR . . . Expansion

Ask students to research one vacation destination that is popular with ecotourists. They can write a short description of the place and how it is helping the local community and the environment (adding a photo if possible) and use the information and photo to make a classroom display.

30 mins

Viewing: Galápagos Tourism *(page 102)*

Overview of the Video

The video presents some information about tourism in the Galápagos Islands.

Vocabulary Notes

vehicle = car, bus, etc.
emissions = carbon dioxide produced by burning gasoline
corporation = company
ruin = destroy

Before Viewing

Exercise A. | Using a Dictionary

- Point out the location of the Galápagos Islands on the global map. Which country are they near? (Ecuador)
- Ask students what they know about the Galápagos Islands and why people go there. (The photo is a clue: to look at marine and other animal life.)
- Have students work individually to read the paragraph and match the words and their definitions.
- Write the answers on the board.
- Ask some questions about the passage: *Why are the Galápagos Islands famous? Why was tourism encouraged? How did tourism harm the islands? What caused people to change their attitude toward tourism? How has their approach changed?*

Answer Key

1. a wake-up call
2. revenue
3. minimize
4. contaminants

Exercise B. | Thinking Ahead

- After students have discussed in pairs, make a list of their suggestions on the board.
- Do not check answers yet as students will do this when they watch the video.

While Viewing

Play the video while students write short answers to the questions.

After Viewing

Exercise A.

- Have students work in pairs to discuss and compare answers.
- Play the video again if necessary.
- Check the answers.

Answer Key

1. There are many unique animal species there.
2. To open businesses and provide services for the tourists
3. It damaged the natural environment and killed an estimated 60 percent of nearby iguanas.
4. –Ending the use of fossil fuels on the Galápagos in the next decade and using only renewable, non-polluting energy
   –Replacing rusty older oil tanks with modern oil tanks
   –Removing contaminants in the fuel to reduce pollution
   –Building an ultra-modern gas station that has barriers to contain leaks
   –Converting boat engines to cleaner and more efficient engines
   –Replacing cars on the islands with low-emissions vehicles
   –Teaching the local community to reduce waste by recycling

Exercise B. | Critical Thinking: Synthesizing

Remind students that connecting information from different sources will help them to remember and understand new information.

Answer Key

Possible answers:
Have stricter rules over where tourists can go and what they can do. Educate tourists and tour companies so they can limit the damage they cause.

IDEAS FOR . . . Checking Comprehension

Ask these additional questions about the video, or write them on the board.

1. How far are the islands from the mainland? (1000 kilometers, or 600 miles)
2. How many people lived on the islands in the 1980s? (About 3000 people)
3. How many people live on the islands today? (More than 25,000 people)
4. What is one international organization that is helping to limit the impact of tourism? (The World Wildlife Fund)
5. Some people argue that humans should not be allowed to visit the islands. Do you agree or disagree? Explain why.

30 mins

Preparing to Read *(page 103)*

WARM-UP

Lesson B target vocabulary is presented in the context of three different programs that attempt to manage environmentally sustainable tourism.

Ask students if they have ever been on a trip to any remote places. Where did they go? What did they do there? What kinds of facilities were available there? How would they evaluate its environmental impact and benefit to the local community?

Exercise A. | Building Vocabulary

- Ask students to choose if they want to work individually or in pairs.
- Explain that students should check the meaning in the passage first, before trying to match the words and the definitions.
- Point out that identifying the part of speech first will help students to find the answers more easily.

Answer Key

1. facilities	**6.** accommodate
2. interpret	**7.** fees
3. self-sufficient	**8.** predominantly
4. dramatically	**9.** dominated
5. pose	**10.** incentive

Exercise B. | Using Vocabulary

- Remind students to use the target words in their answers if possible.
- Discuss the answers as a class.
- Draw students' attention to the **Word Link** box. Ask students to make up sentences using these expressions.

Exercise C. | Brainstorming

- Ask students to work in pairs. They can gather their ideas in a concept map or a chart.
- Write on the board any new vocabulary that comes up.
- Ask each pair to present their ideas to the class.

TIP **Put students into small groups and assign a different type of resort destination to each group. Tell each group to describe their resort location (rainforest, beach, mountain, tropical island) and the type of resort (hotel, guest house, campsite, activity center). Then encourage students to list the ways they would try to benefit the environment and minimize the environmental impact.**

Exercise D. | Predicting

- Ask students to look at the photos and the captions as well as the title and the headings.
- Note: Students will check their predictions after reading in more detail.

track 1-10

You may want to play the audio while students read. Point out the footnotes at the bottom of pages 104–106, and remind students that the notes are there to help them understand the reading.

Overview of the Reading

The reading describes three different programs—in Ecuador, Nepal, and Australia—that have been started by local people in an attempt to develop tourism that benefits their environment and also the local community.

Vocabulary Notes

innovative (paragraph A) = original, new
cabin (paragraph C) = small hut, usually made of wood
animal trap (paragraph C) = device for catching animals
toxic (paragraph D) = poisonous
deforestation (paragraph D) = cutting down trees
threat (paragraph D) = danger
run (a restaurant) (paragraph E) = manage
empower (paragraph F) = make powerful
counterpart (paragraph G) = someone with the same job
trailblazing (paragraph M) = pioneering, never having been done before

Note: Some additional vocabulary items will be studied in exercise **B** on page 107.

IDEAS FOR . . . Checking Comprehension

Ask these additional questions about the reading, or write them on the board.

1. What first motivated the people in each of these stories to start their program? (Huaorani Ecolodge: income and an incentive for the local community to protect the environment; 3 Sisters: local women are given employment opportunities, and female trekkers are given the choice of female guides; Anangu Tours: profits are contributed to local recreation and educational facilities, and the first Aboriginal secondary school was established.)
2. How has tourism changed the environment and the community in each of the places? (Huaorani Ecolodge: dangers recognized to the local culture through the encroachment of the oil industry; 3 Sisters: female trekkers complained of poor treatment by male porters; Anangu Tours: visitors weren't experiencing Aboriginal culture and respecting local traditions.)
3. Which of these places would you most like to visit and why?

45 mins

Understanding the Reading
(pages 107–108)

Check students' predictions in exercise **D** on page 103.

Answer Key

1. Ecuador, Nepal, and Australia
2. They are places of natural beauty that are endangered by tourism.

Exercise A. | Identifying Main Ideas

Check the answers and ask what these three organizations have in common. (They were all started by local people and have the goal of protecting or improving their local environment and community.)

Answer Key

1. c **2.** a **3.** b

Exercise B. | Identifying Meaning from Context

- This exercise has four steps. First, students find and underline the words in the passage.
- Second, they figure out what the words mean in context.
- Third, they complete the definitions.
- Fourth, they check the meanings in a dictionary.
- Ask students to work in pairs to locate and discuss the meaning of the words.
- Check the answers as a class.

Answer Key

1. n., invasion
2. n., accommodation
3. n., handmade objects
4. n., climbers, hikers
5. v., started
6. n., training program
7. n., businesspeople
8. n., representative

Exercise C. | Identifying Supporting Details

- Tell students to locate the paragraphs that contain the answers to these questions. Then ask them to underline the relevant information.
- Discuss the answers as a class.

Answer Key

1. It provides an income and stops commercial tour companies from causing more damage.
2. They can buy locally made handicrafts and learn about rainforest survival skills and medicinal plants.
3. Deforestation, road building, and development

(continued)

Answer Key *(Continued)*

4. They learn to be trekking guides. They learn English conversation. They learn about leadership, health, nutrition, ecological awareness, and conservation.
5. Some program graduates use their earnings to continue their education, while others start their own businesses.
6. Anangu Tours does not let visitors climb the rock.
7. The company contributes profits to local recreation and education facilities and has helped establish the first Aboriginal secondary school in the area.

Exercise D. | Identifying Causes and Effects

- Remind students of the importance of connecting causes and effects to understand a reading.
- Ask them to identify any other causes and effects in the reading.

Answer Key

Cause	Effect
Female trekkers complained of poor treatment by male porters.	The sisters got the idea to start their own business.
3 Sisters Adventure Trekking started EWN	They empower women to be independent, confident, and self-sufficient.

Exercise E. | Critical Thinking: Making Inferences

- Give pairs a few minutes to talk about the questions before leading a class discussion. Remind students that they will need to "read between the lines."

Answer Key

Possible answers:

1. The land belongs to them and the tourists are foreigners.
2. It is sacred. Climbing it is disrespectful.

Exercise F. | Critical Thinking: Synthesizing

- You may want to divide your class into three groups and assign one program to each group.
- Ask them to list: 1. how the program protects the environment 2. how it benefits the local community 3. how it benefits the local culture and traditions.

Exercise G. | Discussing Ideas

- Students may want to discuss places in their country or in other countries that they have visited.
- Lead a class discussion to allow students to share their ideas.

45 mins

Exploring Written English *(pages 109–110)*

Exercise A. | Brainstorming

- Read aloud the writing goal.
- Brainstorm a few ideas as a class. Then ask students to continue in pairs.
- Go over the information in the box about **Free Writing.**
- Set a time limit of five minutes for students to free write.

Exercise B.

- Go over the information and examples in the box.
- Ask students to study the examples and try to paraphrase them. What tense is each verb in?
- Ask them to turn each sentence into its negative form. For example, *If tourism is not managed well, tourists and local people suffer.*
- Allow time for students to complete their answers individually.
- Invite volunteers to write their answers on the board. Make sure punctuation is correct.

Answer Key

1. If you buy local handicrafts [cause], you support the local economy [effect].
2. Forests and beaches can be ruined [effect] if too many people visit them [cause].
3. More women can enjoy trekking [effect] if the porters are female [cause].
4. Tourists can learn about local customs [effect] if they stay at Huaorani Ecolodge [cause].

Exercise C.

Monitor students as they write. Then call on volunteers to read out their most interesting sentences.

Writing Skill: Writing Well-Developed Body Paragraphs

- Go over the information in the box.
- Check comprehension by asking what the purpose of a body paragraph is. (To support the thesis statement and give details about the main idea)

Exercise D. | Critical Thinking: Analyzing

- Go over the task and make sure students understand its purpose. (To see where additional information could be added to make the argument more detailed and convincing)
- Check the answers by reading the questions aloud and calling on students to answer them.
- As additional practice, ask students to rewrite the paragraph in their notebooks, including the additional information.
- To follow up, ask students to choose a paragraph from the reading on pages 104–106 and say what questions it answers.

Answer Key

c. How much has disappeared?
b. How did the community benefit?
a. How many more visitors were there?
d. Who did they partner with?
e. How did they make the park more attractive to tourists?

Writing Task: Drafting

(page 111)

Exercise A. | Planning

- Point out that this planning chart is a useful way to organize ideas before writing.
- Go over the five steps in this exercise.
- Allow time for students to complete their charts, using ideas from exercise **A** and **Free Writing** as appropriate.
- Move around the class while students are writing, offering help and advice as needed.
- Ask one or two students to read their opening sentence aloud.

Exercise B. | Draft 1

- As students write their first draft, walk around and offer help as needed. It is not necessary to correct grammar at this stage.
- You may want to set this task for homework.

Writing Task: Revising

(pages 112–113)

Exercise C. | Critical Thinking: Analyzing

- Explain that analyzing this model essay will help students to revise their own writing.
- Allow time for students to work in pairs.
- Ask students for their opinions about what they liked or disliked in this essay.

Answer Key

1. **Thesis statement:** Local residents are worried that the increased tourism will weaken the local economy and damage the natural beauty of the beaches and the forests.
2. **Two reasons:** Increased tourism will weaken the local economy and damage the natural beauty of the beaches and the forests.
3. **Topic sentences:** 1) Traditional mass tourism can weaken the local economy. 2) Another effect of increased tourism on the northwestern coast is the destruction of the natural beauty of the beaches and the forest.
4. **Key words in topic sentences:** weaken the local economy, destruction of the natural beauty of the beaches and the forest
5. **Details that answer possible reader questions:** (What happens when people stay at big chain hotels?) The money they spend for food and lodging goes to businesses that are probably not locally owned. (What happens if local businesses do not benefit from increased tourism?) If smaller, locally owned businesses aren't successful, they are less able to hire local employees. (How do tourists damage the natural beauty of an area?) They leave garbage everywhere. (What effects does garbage have on an area?) Garbage makes an area look unattractive, and it also harms the local wildlife.
6. Answers will vary.

Exercise D. | Revising

Explain that these steps will help students to reread their work carefully and look for ways to improve it.

Exercise E. | Peer Evaluation

- Explain that this process will help students to see if they have organized their ideas clearly.
- Discuss the four steps in the evaluation process to make sure students know what to do.
- Ensure that both members of the pair have equal time to give feedback.

Writing Task: Editing

(page 114)

Exercise F. | Draft 2

Walk around and monitor students as they work. Provide assistance as needed.

Exercise G. | Editing Practice

- Remind students that the purpose of this exercise is to give them additional practice in editing for grammar in preparation for using the Editing Checklist for their second draft.
- Go over the information in the box.
- Allow time for students to find and correct the mistakes.
- Invite volunteers to write the corrected sentences on the board.

Answer Key

1. **If** prices are too high, people might stop traveling.
2. If travel journalists write about the importance of protecting destinations**,** they educate tourists.
3. If tourists only **eat** at chain restaurants, they don't learn anything about the local food.
4. Tourists are disrespectful of the local **culture if** they climb Ayer's Rock.
5. Local communities can benefit if tourism **promotes** local industries.

Exercise H. | Editing Checklist

- Read the sentences in the Editing Checklist.
- Allow time for students to read and edit their work.

Exercise I. | Final Draft

- Allow time for students to work on their final draft (or set this for homework).
- Collect their work.

IDEAS FOR . . . Further Research

Ask students to research organizations that are helping to promote ecotourism or geotourism. What places do they try to protect? Find some examples of wildlife, natural habitats, and historical places that could benefit from ecotourism. What are some problems with restricting tourism in places that are endangered?

UNIT

Landscape and Imagination

Academic Track
Literature/Humanities

Academic Pathways:
Lesson A: Understanding referencing and cohesion
Understanding figurative language
Lesson B: Interpreting a travel narrative and a novel extract
Lesson C: Writing a concluding paragraph
Writing an explanatory essay

Unit Theme

Unit 6 explores how landscape has inspired the imagination of writers and artists. Topics mentioned in this unit include the Australian outback, Aboriginal rock art, and Route 66—a famous highway in the U.S.

Think and Discuss *(page 115)*

5 mins

- Ask students to describe the photo. Ask: *What makes a city beautiful? What cities in the world do you think are the most beautiful and why?*
- Discuss questions 1 and 2 with the class. Write a list of places on the board. Try to categorize them in terms of their characteristics.

Exploring the Theme *(pages 116–117)*

15 mins

- The opening spread features photos of four very different landscapes.
- Ask students to describe the photos. If possible, locate these places on a global map.
- Write some descriptive adjectives on the board, and ask students which photo(s) they associate with each word. Note that these adjectives will help students to answer question 3. (Possible answers: *lonely, magical, mysterious, remote, intense, exquisite, treacherous, frightening, bleak, magnificent)*
- Have students read the quotations and match them with the photos. Then compare answers as a class.
- Ask students to paraphrase each quotation.
- Point out that the poem by Langston Hughes uses a type of figurative language known as a metaphor in which he imagines the city as a bird. (Figurative language will be studied later in this unit on pages 122 and 131.)
- For question 3, tell students to list adjectives and phrases, or to write a poem.

Answer Key

Possible answers:

1. (1) Boldino, Russia (2) Paris, France (3) Sossusvlei, Namibia (4) Half Dome, California
2. (1) fascinated, inspired (2) affectionate, nostalgic (3) enchanted, spellbound (4) amazed, astonished, overwhelmed
3. Answers will vary.

Notes:

Andrew Wyeth (1917–2009) was a visual artist who created paintings in the realist style. Many of his works were inspired by the people and landscape of his homes in Pennsylvania and Maine. Further information can be found here: http://www.andrewwyeth.com/

Langston Hughes (1902–1967) was an American poet, social activist, novelist, playwright, and columnist. He was part of the Harlem Renaissance, a literary movement of the 1920s centered in the Harlem neighborhood of New York City. Further information can be found here: http://www.biography.com/people/langston-hughes-9346313

Antoine de Saint-Exupéry (1900–1944) was a French writer, poet, and aviator. In the early days of aviation, he flew planes across Africa and once crashed in the Sahara desert, nearly dying of thirst. Further information can be found here: http://www.pbs.org/kcet/chasingthesun/innovators/aexupery.html

Ansel Adams (1902–1984) was an American photographer and environmentalist best known for his black-and-white landscape photographs of the American West, especially Yosemite National Park. Further information can be found here: http://www.sierraclub.org/history/ansel-adams/

30 mins

Preparing to Read *(page 118)*

WARM-UP

The Lesson A target vocabulary is presented in the context of an Australian poet who wrote about the outback.

Ask students what they know about the Australian landscape. What different types of landscape are found there? What dangers and difficulties might be encountered there?

Exercise A. | Building Vocabulary

- Have students find the words in blue in the reading and use the other words around them to guess their meanings.
- Allow time for students to complete the exercise individually.
- Check the answers by asking students to read the sentences aloud.
- Point out the **Word Link** box. Ask students to explain the meaning of these words and to make up sentences using them.
- Tell students to use their dictionaries to find other words using this root—for example, *visual, audiovisual, invisible, visibility, visionary.*

Answer Key

1. h **2.** d **3.** b **4.** e **5.** i **6.** c **7.** a **8.** f **9.** j **10.** g

Exercise B. | Using Vocabulary

- Remind students to use the target words in their discussion.
- Compare answers as a class.
- As a follow-up, ask students to describe well-known places in the world without saying the names. The other students will guess what the places are.

Exercise C. | Brainstorming

You may want to divide students into two groups for this exercise. One group can discuss city life, and the other can discuss country life.

Answer Key

Possible answers: (Answers may depend upon the type of work.)

Working in a Big City	Working in the Country
+ Easier access to transportation, shops, suppliers, customers/ clients + Fees/salaries are higher	+ Cost of living is cheaper, and accommodations are more spacious + There are fewer distractions
– Cost of living and accommodations are more expensive – Conditions are more crowded and noisy	– Difficult to access transportation, shops, suppliers, customers/ clients – Fees/salaries are lower

Exercise D. | Predicting

- Ask students to describe the photo. How might it relate to the title?
- Remind students that *skimming* means reading the first paragraph, the last paragraph, and the first and last lines of every paragraph in between.
- Check the answers after students read in more detail.

track 2-01

You may want to play the audio while students read. Remind them that the vocabulary definitions in the footnotes at the bottom of pages 119–121 will help them understand the reading.

Overview of the Reading

The passage describes a well-known Australian poet named Andrew Paterson who wrote some of Australia's best-loved poems and songs about the Australian outback.

Vocabulary Notes

Ask about or explain the meaning of these additional words in the reading.

outback (title) = countryside, far away from the city
routine (paragraph A) = normal, usual
cattleman (paragraph A) = person whose job is to herd cattle
turn (something) over (to someone) (paragraph A) = refer, give
stern (paragraph A) = strict, severe
chuckle (paragraph B) = gentle laugh
pen name (paragraph C) = name used by a writer in place of his or her real name
bush (paragraph E) = outback
funny (paragraph G) = strange, peculiar

social commentator (paragraph G) = writer, journalist, or broadcaster who writes about society and social behavior
rattling (paragraph G) = shaking, banging, or crashing
picturesque (paragraph G) = pretty

IDEAS FOR . . . Checking Comprehension

Divide the class into two groups. One group will read the verses of the poem about Clancy on page 120. The other group will read the verses of "Waltzing Matilda" on page 121. They will write a paragraph paraphrasing the story in their own words. Then they will form pairs (one partner from each group) and—without looking at the book—retell the story to their partner. The partner can check the details of the story by looking at the book.

IDEAS FOR . . . Expansion

Ask students to research any poets or writers who romanticized life in the wilderness in a similar way—for example, stories about cowboys in the Wild West of North America, about gauchos in Argentina, or about fur trappers in Canada.

45 mins

Understanding the Reading
(page 122)

Check students' predictions in exercise **D** on page 118.

Answer Key

The passage is about Andrew Paterson, an Australian poet who wrote about life in the Australian countryside (outback).

Exercise A. | Identifying Main Ideas

- Ask students to read the sentences. Then have them look back at the passage and identify the correct paragraphs.
- Write the answers on the board.

Answer Key

1. I **2.** K **3.** E **4.** F **5.** D

IDEAS FOR . . . Expansion

As a follow-up, ask students to identify the main idea in the other paragraphs. To make this easier, read out the following sentences or write them on the board. Then ask students to identify the corresponding paragraphs.

1. Australians love to hear stories about life in the bush. (paragraph G)
2. Paterson got the idea for a poem. (paragraph C)
3. "Waltzing Matilda" contains a lot of slang words. (paragraph J)
4. Paterson imagined what Clancy's life was like. (paragraph B)
5. Paterson might have spent his life in the bush. (paragraph H)

Exercise B. | Understanding Similes

- Read the information in the **CT Focus** box.
- Discuss why similes are effective. (They help us visualize images more vividly.)
- Discuss questions 1 and 2 as a class.

Answer Key

1. He compares Melbourne's trams with life in the bush. Australians love to hear about life in the bush, but wouldn't want to live there themselves, just as they like to hear the trams but wouldn't want to ride them.
2. *For Australians, his outback stories were so real they were like childhood memories.* The writer compares Paterson's stories with childhood memories because the stories felt so familiar and people could relate to them easily.

Exercise C. | Identifying Key Details

- Allow time for students to write their answers individually.
- Write the answers on the board.

Answer Key

1. From someone who went away without paying his debts
2. 1889
3. It was the name of a horse that Paterson's family had owned.
4. About 80 percent
5. More than 500

Exercise D. | Discussing Ideas

- For question 1, refer students back to the meaning of the word *inconsistency* in exercise **A** on page 118 (= something that contradicts what you would expect).
- Explain that the word *these* points back to a previous part of the text. (This is known as referencing or cohesion.) The meaning of *these inconsistencies* can be found in paragraph G (= Australians love stories about the outback but wouldn't like to live there).
- For question 2, ask students to identify what Australians found romantic about Clancy's lifestyle. (It was a life surrounded by the natural landscape where you could be independent and free.)

45 mins

Developing Reading Skills
(page 123)

Reading Skill: Understanding Referencing and Cohesion

- Explain that referencing and cohesion are ways of connecting different parts of a text together. It is what makes a paragraph or an essay different from a list of sentences.
- Go over the information in the **Reading Skill** box.
- Point out the difference between subject pronouns (*I, you,* etc.) and possessive pronouns (*mine, yours,* etc.). Both can be used to replace a noun. Examples: *He* is a farmer. The cattle are *his*.
- Explain that possessive adjectives go before a noun—for example: That is *his* farm.
- Study the example. What part of speech is *his*? (Possessive adjective) How do we know that *his* refers to Clancy and not to Paterson?

IDEAS FOR . . . Presenting Grammar

Select a person or a thing from the reading passage, and make a sentence about it using pronouns instead of nouns. Students will guess which person or thing you are talking about. Then ask students to make up their own examples for the others in the class to guess (using this reading or a reading in a previous unit).

Examples:
He didn't pay his debts. (Clancy)
He didn't like his job. (Paterson)
They tried to arrest him. (policemen, tramp)
He sang a song to it. (swagman, cooking pot or sheep)

Exercise A. | Applying

- Do the first item with the class as an example. Write the sentence on the board and model how to draw a line from the possessive adjective to the antecedent.
- Allow time for students to read the sentences and discuss their answers in pairs.
- Remind students that the antecedent has to agree in number and gender with the reference word and also has to make sense in the context.

Answer Key

1. his → cattleman, their → creditors
2. his → Clancy, their → creditors, their → creditors and lawyers
3. his → Paterson, it → free life in the bush, his → Paterson
4. It → the poem "Clancy of the Overflow"

Exercise B. | Applying

Point out that this exercise has two steps. First, check that students have underlined the correct words. Then have students circle the antecedents.

Answer Key

1. his → Banjo Paterson **2.** he → Banjo Paterson **3.** his → Banjo Paterson **4.** he → Banjo Paterson **5.** he → Banjo Paterson **6.** his → Banjo Paterson **7.** they → stories **8.** they → stories **9.** their → Australians today

IDEAS FOR . . . Expansion

Ask students to select another paragraph from the reading passage and identify all the pronouns and possessive adjectives and their antecedents. Monitor students as they work and pick out any possibly confusing examples to discuss with the class.

30 mins

Viewing: Rock Artists of Australia *(page 124)*

Overview of the Video

The video presents some information about aboriginal rock art in the past and today.

Vocabulary Notes

spring (past: *sprang*) = emerge, originate
untold = countless, innumerable
time-honored = traditional
chances are = it is likely
ochre = reddish-yellow earth used for painting
clay = sticky earth used for making pots or bricks

Before Viewing

Exercise A. | Using a Dictionary

- Ask students what they know about Aborigines in Australia. What do they know about the history of Australia? What do they know about aboriginal culture? Refer them to the reading passage on page 106 in Unit 5 for some ideas.
- Ask students to describe the photo. What type of art is shown here? How was it made? What does it depict?
- Have students work individually to match the words and their definitions.
- Write the answers on the board.
- Ask students to predict how these words will be used in the video.

Answer Key

1. creation **2.** aboriginal **3.** portable **4.** bark **5.** impart **6.** clan

Exercise B. | Thinking Ahead

After students have discussed in pairs, make a list of their suggestions on the board.

While Viewing

- Play the video while students write short answers to the questions.

Note: The *Dreamtime* (or the *Dreaming*) is a system of beliefs of the aboriginal Australians consisting of legends and stories about ancient spirits that created the world. These beliefs embody a profound respect for nature and establish the patterns of life for aboriginal society and the ceremonies that are to be performed to preserve the balance of nature and ensure continuity of life.

After Viewing

Exercise A.

- Have students work in pairs to discuss and compare answers.
- Play the video again if necessary.
- Check the answers.

Answer Key

1. The dreamtime
2. Animal, birds, and fish
3. Certain clans were responsible for painting specific animals, such as turtles.
4. Bark, paper, and wood
5. They are gradually being eroded by rain, insects, and reptiles.

Exercise B. | Synthesizing

Use students' answers to reach a definition of the term *national identity.* This may include history, language, art, poetry, or music.

IDEAS FOR . . . Checking Comprehension

Ask these additional questions about the video, or write them on the board. (Note that questions 4 and 5 require making some inferences.)

1. How long have the aboriginal people inhabited this country? (Forty thousand or maybe a hundred thousand years)
2. Which animals are mentioned or shown? (Kangaroos, birds, fish, turtles)
3. What were the purposes of the paintings? (To tell their history, to ask for a good harvest, and as part of a magical ceremony to keep the earth healthy)
4. Why do you think the artists' work is now valuable? (There are few people left who are skilled in making such paintings.)
5. What conflicts do you think there may be between the aboriginal way of life and modern-day culture? (Modern urban culture does not respect the land, nature, or animals. It creates pollution and damages the environment.)

30 mins

Preparing to Read *(page 125)*

WARM-UP

Lesson B target vocabulary is presented in the context of the history of Route 66 and how it has been reflected in American popular culture.

Ask students if they have ever been on a road trip. Where did they go? What did they enjoy about it?

Have students study the graphics on page 128. What type of information is presented there? How is it presented?

Exercise A. | Building Vocabulary

- Ask students to choose if they want to work individually or in pairs.
- Point out that identifying the part of speech first will help them to find the answers more easily.

Answer Key

1. define	**6.** possessions
2. parade	**7.** vanishing
3. precious	**8.** abandon
4. legendary	**9.** migrant
5. attraction	**10.** celebrate

Exercise B. | Using Vocabulary

- Ask students to work in pairs or small groups. Encourage students to try to establish criteria for each question. For example, *What makes something valuable?* (Monetary value, personal associations, beauty) *What makes a place attractive to tourists?* (Beauty, history) *What make a person legendary?* (Fame, talent, success)
- Ask a few pairs/groups to share their ideas with the class.
- Draw students' attention to the **Word Link** box. Ask students to find definitions for each of these words. Ask: *What is migration? What are some reasons that humans, animals, and birds migrate?*

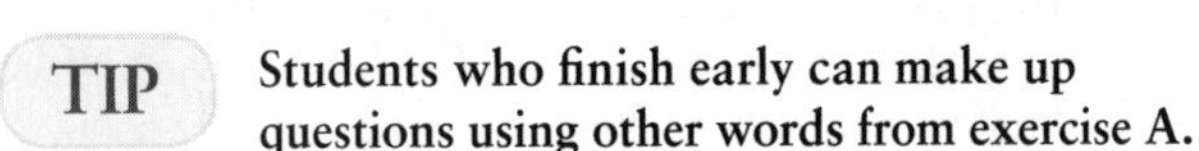

TIP **Students who finish early can make up questions using other words from exercise A. They can ask their partner or write them on the board for everyone to answer.**

Exercise C. | Brainstorming

This may be easier to discuss if students think of a specific road that is well known in their country.

Answer Key

Possible answers:

Scenic views, connects important places, historical associations

Exercise D. | Predicting

- Ask students to look at the photos and the captions as well as the title and the headings.
- There is no need to check the answers now. This will be done after students have finished reading the passage in detail.

track 2-02

You may want to play the audio while students read. Point out the vocabulary definitions in the footnotes at the bottom of pages 126, 127, and 129.

Overview of the Reading

The reading describes some of the history of Route 66 and how it has inspired writers, artists, and musicians over the years.

Vocabulary Notes

multilane (paragraph A) = many lanes
rootless (paragraph B) = not tied down
stretch (paragraph C) = section of road
embrace (paragraph C) = hug
Okies (paragraph D) = people from Oklahoma
Dust Bowl (paragraph D) = farmland severely affected by drought in the 1930s
servicemen (paragraph D) = military
boarded up (paragraph E) = closed
in the grip of (paragraph K) = suffering from
refugees (paragraph M) = people fleeing persecution or poverty

IDEAS FOR . . . Checking Comprehension

Ask students to paraphrase these lines in their own words.

1. I know we're living in yesterday here. (paragraph F) (Possible answer: I know we're pretending life is as easy as it used to be.)
2. This is where you go looking for who we used to be. (paragraph F) (Possible answer: This is the place you go to pretend that not much has changed.)
3. They are modern-day pilgrims. (paragraph H) (Possible answer: They are people looking for a better life.)
4. This is the crossroads of the world. (paragraph H) (Possible answer: This is where people of the world meet in the same place.)

45 mins

Understanding the Reading *(pages 130–131)*

Check students' predictions in exercise **D** on page 125.

Answer Key

It may be called "the mother road" because it generated many stories and legends, or because it led the way to new opportunities. It's special as a symbol of our nation's past.

Exercise A. | Identifying Main Ideas

Call on students to read the sentences aloud.

Answer Key

1. favorite, all things were possible
2. settled on, left
3. the road, the dream
4. Great Depression, life, Okies/migrants

Exercise B. | Identifying Meaning from Context

- Check the answers as a class.
- Discuss any other meanings of these words: *trace* can also be a verb that means "to search for something"; *stream* can also mean "a small river."

Answer Key

1. noun, something placed instead of another thing
2. noun, sign or clue
3. adjective, spooky, scary, strange
4. noun, river, nonstop traffic

Exercise C. | Identifying Supporting Details

- Tell students to underline the relevant information.
- Discuss the answers as a class.

Answer Key

People who traveled on Route 66:
1930s: migrants fleeing the drought
1940s: soldiers going home or going to war
1950s: young people looking for adventure

Where is Route 66?
- Chicago
- Los Angeles
- 2,500
- eight

How is it celebrated?
Song: "Get Your Kicks on Route 66"
Novels: *The Grapes of Wrath* by John Steinbeck, *On the Road* by Jack Kerouac
TV/Movie: *Route 66*

Exercise D. | Identifying Key Details

- Point out that the time line arrow goes from left to right and each date is attached to the time line in order. Ask: *How many pieces of information do you need to find?* (Five) *What kind of reading skill will you use to find this information?* (Scanning)
- Draw the time line on the board, and call on students to complete the missing information.
- Have them add other dates from the reading.

Answer Key

1954: Harvey House Hotel closed
1957: novel *On the Road* was published
1959: author first traveled the road
Early 1960s: TV show *Route 66*
1984: replacement road was completed

Exercise E. | Critical Thinking: Understanding Figurative Language

- Go over the information in the **CT Focus** box.
- Refer students to the information about similes on page 122 and the poem by Langston Hughes on page 117. Ask what kind of figurative language is used there.
- Do the first item together. Ask: *Does it use the word* like *or* as*? Does it give human characteristics to an object?*
- Ask students to find other examples of figurative language in the passage.

Answer Key

1. P **2.** P **3.** S **4.** M **5.** P **6.** P

Exercise F. | Critical Thinking: Synthesizing

Emphasize the importance of not just understanding information, but connecting it to other information.

Answer Key

Possible answers:

1. The author feels nostalgia for the romance and freedom of automobile travel in the 1950s. (paragraph B) in love with the open road, the excitement of being alone and rootless and going someplace, anyplace; (paragraph C) I feel as though I have returned to the embrace of a friend.
2. Steinbeck's style is direct and naturalistic. It conveys what life was like at that time. Paterson's poetry is highly stylized, creating a picture that is romantic and attractive but not necessarily truthful.

45 mins

Exploring Written English *(pages 132–134)*

TIP As preparation for this lesson, you may want to bring in a selection of classic books or well-known stories in English and have students choose one to talk about in the next class.

Exercise A. | Brainstorming

- Read the writing goal aloud.
- Brainstorm a few ideas as a class. Then ask students to continue in pairs. (The books, stories, or movies can be in English or in students' own language.)
- Go over the information in the box about **Free Writing.**
- Set a time limit of five minutes for students to free write.

Exercise B.

- Go over the information and examples in the **Language for Writing** box.
- Ask students to study the examples. Can they rephrase each example as two sentences?
- Mention that appositive phrases can be at the beginning or end of a sentence, or in the middle. Point out the use of commas in appositive phrases.
- Allow time for students to complete their answers individually.
- Invite volunteers to write their answers on the board.

Answer Key

1. *The Casual Vacancy* is an adult novel by J. K. Rowling, a successful author of children's books.
2. Rowling is best known for creating Harry Potter, the main character in her best-selling series.
3. A lot can be learned from *To Kill a Mockingbird*, a novel about injustice and prejudice.
4. Harper Lee, an American author, wrote *To Kill a Mockingbird.*
5. The movie version of *To Kill a Mockingbird* stars Gregory Peck, a very successful American actor.

Writing Skill: Writing a Concluding Paragraph

- Go over the information in the box.
- Ask: *What is the purpose of a concluding paragraph? What are three ways to make a restatement or paraphrase? What are two ways to leave the reader with a final thought?*

Exercise C. | Applying

- Go over the task and make sure students understand its purpose. (To practice paraphrasing)
- Monitor students as they write. Then call on volunteers to read the completed sentences aloud.

Answer Key

1. important, characters
2. Music, issues, entertainment
3. teach, society, entertains
4. strong, as

Exercise D. | Applying

- Go over the task and make sure students understand its purpose (to practice ways of leaving the reader with a final thought).
- Check the answers by reading the questions and calling on students to answer them.

TIP Lower-level students can complete two sentences, while higher-level students can make predictions and rhetorical sentences about all four sentences.

Writing Task: Drafting

(page 135)

Exercise A. | Planning

- Point out that this planning chart is a useful way to organize ideas before writing.
- Go over the five steps in the exercise.
- Allow time for students to complete their charts, using ideas from exercise **A** and **Free Writing** as appropriate.
- Move around the class while students are writing, offering help and advice as needed.
- Ask one or two students to read their opening sentence aloud.

Exercise B. | Draft 1

- As students write their first draft, walk around and offer help as needed. It is not necessary to correct grammar at this stage.
- You may want to set this task for homework.

Writing Task: Revising

(pages 136–137)

Exercise C. | Critical Thinking: Analyzing

- Explain that analyzing this model essay will help students to revise their own writing.
- Allow time for students to work in pairs.
- Ask students for their opinions about what they liked or disliked in this essay.

Answer Key

1. **Thesis statement:** However, with some movies, the story could not happen in any other city.
2. **Topic sentences:** 1) Most of the important events in the movie involve travel back in time, to Paris in the early twentieth century. 2) Another important event in the movie is Gil's decision to break up with Inez and stay in Paris.
3. **Answer reader questions:** Possible answers: 1) One night, … an old car stops in front of him. The driver and passengers … invite him to come with them. (How does Gil travel in time?) 2) However, after his experiences with the artists and writers of Paris's past, Gil finds the strength to leave Inez and stay in Paris. (How/Why does Gil decide to break up with Inez?)
4. **Summary statement:** *Midnight in Paris* could not be set in any other city.
5. **Final thought:** Haven't you ever wanted to live in a different time and place, and wondered how it might change your life?

Exercise D. | Revising

Explain that these steps will help students to reread their work carefully and look for ways to improve it.

Exercise E. | Peer Evaluation

- Discuss the four steps in the evaluation process to make sure students know what to do.
- Ensure that both members of the pair have equal time to give feedback.

Exercise F. | Draft 2

Walk around and monitor students as they work. Provide assistance as needed.

Writing Task: Editing

(page 138)

Exercise G. | Editing Practice

- Go over the information in the box.
- Allow time for students to find and correct the mistakes.
- Invite volunteers to write the corrected sentences on the board.

Answer Key

1. Shanghai**, a major financial center**, has a larger population than any other city.
2. *Temptress Moon***, a film by director Chen Kaige,** is set in Shanghai.
3. The star of the film, **Gong Li**, had worked with the director in a previous film.
4. *Farewell My Concubine***, Chen Kaige and Gong Li's previous film**, was made in 1993.
5. Gong Li's first film, ***Red Sorghum***, was the first film by director Zhang Yimou.

Exercise H. | Editing Checklist

- Read the sentences in the Editing Checklist.
- Allow time for students to read and edit their work.

Exercise I. | Final Draft

- Allow time for students to work on their final draft (or set this for homework).
- Collect their work.

IDEAS FOR . . . Further Research

Ask students to choose one movie that is based on a book. They will write an essay on the way landscape or setting is used differently in the book and in the movie, and say which was better and why.

Ask students to choose one artist or photographer who uses landscape in his or her work. They will write an essay explaining how the artist uses landscape and how it influences the work.

Global Appetites

Academic Track
Interdisciplinary

Academic Pathways:
Lesson A: Interpreting visual information
Inferring a writer's tone and purpose
Lesson B: Understanding an environmental report
Lesson C: Using an outline to plan an essay
Writing a persuasive essay

Unit Theme

Unit 7 explores the impact that humans are having on the environment and the steps that need to be taken to ensure a sustainable future for our planet.

Think and Discuss *(page 139)*

5 mins

- Ask students to describe the photo: *What can you see in the photo? What activity is going on here? Where can you find places like this?*
- Discuss the difference between products and natural resources, and give or elicit some examples of each.
- Together with the class, write two lists on the board in answer to questions 1 and 2.
- Discuss the meaning of the unit title and how it might relate to the photo.

Exploring the Theme *(pages 140–141)*

15 mins

- The opening spread features a world map showing the growth in GDP (gross domestic product) of countries around the world.
- Ask students what they notice about the map. (The countries are not in the usual geographical scale in relation to one another.)
- Explain the difference between production and consumption, and explain that one way to measure consumption is to look at GDP (because production uses up resources).
- Ask students to read the information and study the map.
- Discuss question 1 and ask some additional questions: *What do the black dots represent? What do the white dots represent? What do the large yellow numbers represent?*
- Discuss questions 2 and 3. (For question 2, students will need to look at the total number of black dots and at the colors. For question 3, they will need to look at the large yellow numbers as well as the number of white dots in relation to black dots.)
- Discuss why some countries are growing quickly and some are not. What prevents an economy from growing? Is economic growth always a good thing? What are the advantages and disadvantages of growth?
- Lead into a more general discussion of why there are inequalities in wealth between different parts of the world.

Answer Key

Possible answers:

1. The country's size represents its total GDP (gross domestic product). The color represents the GDP per person.
2. The U.S. and Japan are consuming the most. The U.S., Singapore, Norway, and parts of the Middle East consume the most per person.
3. The fastest rise in consumption is in China followed by India.

IDEAS FOR . . . Expansion

Ask students to make a list of all the things they spend money on in one month and estimate how much they spend on each one. What proportion of their consumption is spent on the following: food, transportation, education, communication, entertainment? They can present the results in the form of a pie chart or a bar graph. What did everyone have in common?

Ask students to discuss what goods they feel they (or people generally) consume too much of and how they could try to reduce their consumption or persuade other people to reduce theirs.

30 mins

Preparing to Read *(page 142)*

WARM-UP

The Lesson A target vocabulary is presented in the context of problems caused by the Earth's growing population and consequent overconsumption of resources.

Ask students what they know about world population. How big is it? Why is it growing? Which countries are growing the most and the fastest? What are some of the problems caused by population growth?

Exercise A. | Building Vocabulary

- Have students find the words in blue in the reading and use the other words around them to guess their meanings.
- Remind students that looking at the part of speech can help them figure out the meaning.
- Allow time for students to complete the exercise individually.
- Point out the **Word Partners** box. Ask students to explain the meaning of these phrases.

Vocabulary Note

Note that *goods* is usually used in the plural form. In general English, it means property or possessions. In economics, it refers to things that are produced (in contrast to *services,* which are not physical things). The singular form (*a good*) is sometimes used in economics. Goods are often divided into *durable* goods (such as computers and TVs) and *nondurable* goods (such as food).

TIP **Ask students for other word forms of the verb *consume* (*consumer, consumption, consumerism*). Ask: *What kinds of things can you consume?* (time, energy, money, resources, food) Ask: *In what ways are we a consumer society? What is consumer confidence? Why is it important?***

Answer Key

1. initially	**6.** intensive
2. output	**7.** consume
3. accessible	**8.** vehicle
4. goods	**9.** commerce
5. obvious	**10.** overall

Exercise B. | Using Vocabulary

- Remind students to use the target words in their discussion.
- Compare answers as a class.

Exercise C. | Brainstorming

- Put students into groups and ask each group to prepare an idea map on a large poster outlining their answers to these three questions.
- Have students present their idea maps to the class.

Answer Key

Possible answers:

1. and **2.** Renewable resources: water, air, sunlight, wind energy, trees; Nonrenewable resources: oil, coal, natural gas
3. There will be shortages of food, energy, clean water, clean air.

Exercise D. | Predicting

- Ask students to describe the photos. How do they relate to the title?
- Check the answers after students read the passage.
- Note that the chart on page 145 will be studied in exercise **B** on page 148.

track **2-03**

You may want to play the audio while students read. Remind them that the vocabulary definitions in the footnotes at the bottom of pages 143 and 144 will help them understand the reading.

Overview of the Reading

The passage describes some of the problems that are caused by the overconsumption of resources.

Vocabulary Notes

Ask about or explain the meaning of these additional words in the reading.

strain (title) = stretch, put under pressure
footprint (paragraph A) = literally, the mark or outline left by a foot on the ground; in this context, the impact of humans on the environment, the amount of resources they consume (ecological footprint)
breaking point (paragraph A) = crisis point, the point at which something gives way
quadrupled (paragraph B) = multiplied by four
astounding (paragraph C) = astonishing, amazing
scarce (paragraph D) = not easily available, difficult to find
clear (paragraph E) = cut down
livestock (paragraph F) = cattle, farm animals
heat-trapping gases (paragraph F) = gases that trap heat in the atmosphere, such as CFCs (chlorofluorocarbons)
scope (paragraph G) = extent or range
all along (paragraph G) = all this time up to now

IDEAS FOR . . . Checking Comprehension

Ask students the following questions about the reading, or write them on the board.

1. What are the causes of overconsumption, according to the author? (Increasing population, economic growth, industrialization, and globalization)
2. What suggestions does the author make for using fewer resources in the future? (Find new sources of non-polluting energy, recycle and reuse, conserve more and consume fewer resources, manage the water supply)

IDEAS FOR . . . Expansion

- Ask students to research different methods of measuring our ecological footprint. They can search the Internet using key words: *ecological footprint calculator*
  Some websites:
  http://www.earthday.org/footprint-calculator
  http://www.myfootprint.org/
  http://www.footprintnetwork.org/
- Ask students to research facts and information about the growth of the world's population.

Understanding the Reading

45 mins

(pages 146–147)

Check students' predictions in exercise **D** on page 142.

Answer Key

The correct answer is c (problems that are caused by the overconsumption of resources). The passage does not suggest reducing population growth (b). Ways to use fewer resources (a) are mentioned only briefly in the last paragraph.

Exercise A. | Identifying Main Ideas

- Ask students to read the sentences. Then have them look back at the passage and reread the relevant paragraphs.
- Check the answers and ask students to explain their choices by referring to the text.
- Write the answers on the board.

Answer Key

1. a **2.** b **3.** a **4.** a **5.** b

Exercise B. | Identifying Key Details

- Allow time for students to write their answers individually.
- Write the answers on the board.

Answer Key

1. fewer large fish, damaged fertile soil, atmosphere filled with greenhouse gases
2. The world economy and industrial output have grown, there is more irrigated land
3. Over the past few decades
4. Fewer supplies
5. Rising demand for luxury foods such as seafood and beef
6. Basic goods and luxuries; food, energy, water
7. Fresh water

Exercise C. | Critical Thinking: Understanding Tone and Purpose

- Go over the information in the **CT Focus** box. Explain that a writer's tone and purpose can be *inferred* from the type of language he or she uses, and are not usually directly stated. The writer chooses certain words or expressions because they have positive or negative connotations and will persuade the reader to agree with his or her point of view.
- For item 1, discuss the writer's choice of the word *heavy.* What does it imply? (It implies that humans have a serious and harmful impact on the Earth's environment.)
- Tell students to continue the exercise in pairs and to explain in each case what the choice of words implies.

Answer Key P147

1. heavy, greed, to its breaking point
2. **B:** have disappeared, has been damaged, has been filled with greenhouse gases
   E: emptied of fish, cleared to raise cattle
   F: fill the air with heat-trapping gases, of waste
3. concerned, serious
4. *We will need to* is repeated four times. The author's purpose is to persuade the reader that action is necessary and urgent.

Exercise D. | Critical Thinking: Evaluating an Argument

- Encourage students to think of counterarguments to those presented in the passage. For example, advances in renewable energy sources and improved methods of managing fish supplies will make the situation less serious in the future.

- Lead into a general discussion of whether developed countries should share more of the burden for the depletion of world resources and for pollution and climate change.

45 mins

Developing Reading Skills *(page 148)*

Reading Skill: Interpreting Visual Information

- Explain that understanding charts and diagrams is an important reading skill.
- Go over the information in the **Reading Skill** box.
- Ask students to look back through the book and find some other examples of maps, graphs, charts, or diagrams.
- Ask some questions to check comprehension: *What does the title of a graph tell you? What does the axis tell you? What does the length of each bar represent?*
- Note that bar graphs generally have two axes, the horizontal axis (along the bottom) and the vertical axis (along the side).

TIP **You may want to practice some useful language for talking about bar graphs. For example, *The graph shows/depicts/compares/illustrates . . ., Each bar represents . . ., The height of each bar indicates . . .***

Exercise A. | Interpreting Bar Graphs

- Questions 1 and 2 help students to understand the information in the bar graph. Question 3 helps them to evaluate the information.

Answer Key

1. The bar graphs show the amount of global grain trade according to country.
2. Each bar represents how much grain each country imports or exports. The numbers mean total millions of metric tons per year (annually).
3. Answers will vary.

- Write the following additional questions on the board for students to discuss in pairs.

1. *What is the purpose of these bar graphs?* (To compare countries according to how much grain they import or export)
2. *What is the horizontal axis?* (Countries)
3. *What is the vertical axis?* (Millions of metric tons annually)
4. *How are these two graphs organized?* (The bars are organized from left to right according to size.)
5. *What do the colors represent?* (Blue represents major importers, and orange represents major exporters.)

Exercise B. | Critical Thinking: Interpreting Visual Information

- Refer students back to page 145.
- Ask some general questions about the chart. For example, *What is the title? What does the legend tell you? What is the vertical axis? What is the horizontal axis? How is the graph organized? What conclusions can be drawn from the graph?*
- Allow time for students to discuss in pairs. Write helpful language on the board if appropriate.
- Have students ask each other additional questions about the graph.

Answer Key

1. The graph shows how much water is required to produce each type of food product. Each blue dot indicates 10 liters.
2. It takes 3,400 liters (898 gallons) of water to produce 1 kilogram or 2.2 pounds of rice.
3. If fewer people ate meat (or if people ate less meat), we would use less water.

IDEAS FOR . . . Expansion

Ask students to select another graph from this book (for example, page 94) and answer the same questions about it. They can work in pairs or groups to write a description and an interpretation as a short paragraph. Then have some students read their paragraphs aloud to the class.

30 mins

Viewing: The Greendex

(page 149)

Overview of the Video

The video describes a way of measuring consumer behavior known as the Greendex. It was developed as a way to find out what impact countries are having on the environment.

Vocabulary Note

Thermal imaging cameras can detect infrared radiation and produce images of it. The amount of radiation emitted by an object increases with temperature, so thermal imaging allows us to see variations in temperature.

Before Viewing

Exercise A. | Using a Dictionary

- Ask students to describe the photo. Discuss what a thermal image shows. Look back at page 145 at another example of a thermal image.
- Have students work individually to match the words and their definitions.
- Write the answers on the board.
- Ask students to predict how these words will be used in the video.

Answer Key

1. reversible **2.** components **3.** came in last **4.** energy efficiency **5.** index

Exercise B. | Thinking Ahead

Discuss what kinds of things we use every day that consume energy. Which ones consume the most energy? Which ones are most or least energy efficient? How would you find out how energy efficient your kitchen appliances are?

While Viewing

Play the video while students write short answers to the questions.

After Viewing

Exercise A.

- Have students work in pairs to discuss and compare answers.
- Play the video again if necessary.
- Check the answers.
- Ask students for their opinion of the Greendex. Do they think it is helpful? How could people buy more locally grown food and drive less?

Answer Key

1. Housing, transportation, food, and "goods" (recycling and garbage, consumption of big appliances)
2. Brazil and India. People in these countries have smaller homes. They don't use a lot of fuel, and they don't buy a lot of major appliances.
3. 25 percent
4. Buying locally grown food and driving less

Exercise B. | Synthesizing

- Ask students to role-play a conversation between the author of "Straining Our Resources" and the inventor of the Greendex.
- Write a list of topics on the board to help guide their conversation—for example, *energy, food, water, transportation, recycling.*

IDEAS FOR . . . Checking Comprehension

Ask these additional questions about the video, or write them on the board. (Note that questions 4 and 5 require making some inferences.)

1. What does the Greendex do? (It measures consumer behavior and its impact on the environment.)
2. What aspects of housing does it measure? (The size of homes, how they're heated and cooled, and their energy efficiency)
3. What aspects of transportation does it measure? (How many people own cars and how many people use public transportation)
4. What aspects of food does it measure? (The amounts of local produce, meat, and bottled water people buy)
5. How many countries were surveyed in 2008? (14)

30 mins

Preparing to Read *(page 150)*

WARM-UP

Lesson B target vocabulary is presented in the context of the steps that can be taken for our planet to become more sustainable.

Ask students what types of alternative energy they know about. Which ones have they seen or used?

Exercise A. | Building Vocabulary

- Ask students to choose if they want to work individually or in pairs.
- Remind the class that a word's meaning in context can often be slightly different from the definition in a dictionary.

Answer Key

1. j **2.** c **3.** h **4.** a **5.** d **6.** b **7.** g **8.** f **9.** e **10.** i

TIP Review the target words by having students quiz each other in pairs. One person looks at the book and reads out the definition. The other tries to remember the word.

Exercise B. | Using Vocabulary

- Ask students to work in pairs.
- Have each pair present one idea for each question to the class.
- Draw students' attention to the **Word Partners** box. Ask students to give examples for each phrase.

Exercise C. | Brainstorming

- Draw a chart on the board with one column for problems and one for solutions.
- As a class, make a list of the problems and write them in the chart.
- Have students discuss solutions in pairs.
- Write their ideas in the chart.

Exercise D. | Predicting

- Discuss what students think is meant by the term *sustainable.*
- Ask students to look at the photos and study the map as well as the title and the headings.

track 2-04

You may want to play the audio as students read the passage. Remind students that the footnotes on pages 151, 152, and 154 can help them to better understand the reading.

Overview of the Reading

Whereas the reading passage in Lesson A presents the problems facing a sustainable future, the Lesson B reading describes eight ways in which people around the world are trying to conserve more and consume less in order for Earth to achieve sustainability.

Vocabulary Notes

Ask about or explain the meaning of these additional words in the reading.
restore (paragraph A) = replace
conserve (paragraph C) = use as little as possible without waste
incentives (paragraph E) = something that makes you want to do something
preserve (paragraph J) = save
emissions (paragraph L) = gases that are produced by cars, machines, or factories

Note that more vocabulary from the passage will be studied in exercise **B** on page 155.

IDEAS FOR . . . Checking Comprehension

Ask students these additional questions about the reading. Encourage students to answer with information from the passage as well as their own ideas.

1. What are some other ways to reduce traffic? (paragraph D)
2. What kinds of financial incentives could be introduced? (paragraph E)
3. What are some other examples of renewable energy? (paragraphs F and G)
4. What are other types of companies that socially responsible investors could invest in? (paragraph H)
5. What are some other negative effects of forestry logging? (paragraph J)
6. What are some other examples of green employment? (paragraph K)
7. What are some ways to reduce carbon emissions? (paragraph L)

45 mins

Understanding the Reading *(pages 155–156)*

Exercise A. | Identifying Main Ideas

- Ask students to work individually.
- Call on students to read their answers aloud.

Answer Key

1. protect their local environment and reduce their impact on the global environment
2. moving livestock producers away from the cities
3. create light with less heat, use 75 percent less energy, and last 10 times longer than traditional light bulbs
4. logging is regulated and carried out in a sustainable way
5. measures to cut carbon emissions

Exercise B. | Identifying Meaning from Context

- Ask students to work individually or in pairs to locate and discuss the meaning of the words.
- Check the answers as a class.

Answer Key

1. is
2. deal with, tackle, solve
3. gathering, collecting
4. people whose job is to cut down trees
5. about, approximately

Exercise C. | Interpreting Visual Information

- Refer students to the map on pages 152–153. Ask some general questions: *What is the title? What do the colors represent? What do the colored circles and the numbers represent? What do the black circles and the numbers represent? Describe each type of energy source.*
- Ask students to summarize the information shown in the map.
- Discuss the answers as a class.

Answer Key

1. It shows which countries have renewable energy sources. It relates to step 3.
2. Solar PV and Solar hot water/heat; Solar PV: Germany, Solar hot water/heat: China
3. China and the U.S.

Exercise D. | Identifying Supporting Details

Students can work individually or in pairs.

Answer Key

1. Using solar ovens to cook food
2. Animal waste causes water pollution, animals can spread diseases to humans
3. Wind power
4. Alternative energy production or environmentally sound waste-management practices
5. Japan
6. It contributes to water pollution and leads to the destruction of animal habitats and soil erosion.
7. the renewable-energy industry: production of wind turbines, production of solar energy
8. Costa Rica; it promises zero net carbon emissions by 2030

Exercise E. | Critical Thinking: Understanding Tone and Purpose

Review the information about understanding a writer's tone and purpose on page 147.

Answer Key

1. optimistic, encouraging
2. To give information about how to achieve sustainability
3. Possible answer: The first passage is more persuasive. The second is more factual. The first is more pessimistic. The second is more optimistic.

Exercise F. | Critical Thinking: Evaluating Ideas

Emphasize the importance of not just understanding information, but also connecting it with your own life and comparing it with your experience.

45 mins

Exploring Written English

(pages 157–158)

Exercise A. | Brainstorming

- Read the writing goal aloud.
- Brainstorm a few ideas as a class. Then ask students to continue in pairs.
- Go over the information in the box about **Free Writing**.
- Set a time limit of five minutes for students to free write.

Exercise B.

- Go over the information and examples in the **Language for Writing** box.
- Ask students to study the two examples of restrictive clauses. How are they different?
- Ask students to study the two examples of nonrestrictive clauses. How are they different?
- Refer students to pages 247–248 for more information if necessary.
- Allow time for students to complete their answers individually.
- Invite volunteers to write their answers on the board.
- Ask students if these are restrictive or nonrestrictive clauses. Have them say why.

TIP **To determine whether a clause is restrictive or nonrestrictive, see if the sentence makes sense without the clause. If so, it is a nonrestrictive clause.**

Answer Key

1. The city of Curitiba, which has an efficient bus system, has very little traffic congestion.
2. Sustainability, which means preserving our valuable resources, is the key to our future survival.
3. Earth's renewable resources, which include clean air and water, are becoming scarce.

Writing Skill: Using an Outline to Plan an Essay

- Go over the information in the box.
- Point out the use of Roman numerals and letters to organize the information.
- Ask which sections are written as full statements and which are written as notes.

Exercise C.

Monitor students as they write, and call on volunteers to read out their additional information.

Exercise D. | Critical Thinking: Analyzing

- This task combines all the steps that students have studied in each unit up to now.
- Remind students of the various parts of an essay that they have already studied: opening sentence, thesis statement, topic sentences, supporting details, and concluding paragraph.
- Ask what students can remember about each point. Refer back to information in preceding units if students have difficulty.
- Allow time for students to work in pairs and ask you questions if necessary.

Writing Task: Drafting

(page 159)

Exercise A. | Planning

- Point out that this planning chart is a useful way to organize ideas before writing.
- Go over the five steps in the exercise.
- Allow time for students to complete their charts, using ideas from exercise **A** and **Free Writing** as appropriate.
- Move around the class while students are writing, offering help and advice as needed.
- Ask one or two students to read their thesis statement aloud.

Exercise B. | Draft 1

- As students write their first draft, walk around and offer help as needed. It is not necessary to correct grammar at this stage.
- You may want to set this task for homework.

Writing Task: Revising

(pages 160–161)

Exercise C. | Critical Thinking: Analyzing

- Explain that analyzing this model essay will help students to revise their own writing.
- Allow time for students to work in pairs.
- Ask students for their opinions about what they liked or disliked in this essay.

Answer Key

1. **Thesis statement:** Saving water and slowing down climate change are just two reasons for becoming a vegetarian.
2. **Two reasons:** 1) Saving water 2) slowing down climate change (Yes, Yes)
3. **Topic sentences:** 1) One environmental benefit of being vegetarian is that it saves large amounts of water. 2) Another reason to become a vegetarian is that it helps to slow down global warming.
4. **Key words:** saves large amounts of water, slow down global warming
5. Yes
6. Yes
7. **Questions:** Why does meat production use more water than plants? How does meat production add to global warming?

Exercise D. | Revising

Explain that these steps will help students to reread their work carefully and look for ways to improve it.

Exercise E. | Peer Evaluation

- Explain that this process will help students to see if they have organized their ideas clearly.
- Discuss the four steps in the evaluation process to make sure students know what to do.
- Ensure that both members of the pair have equal time to give feedback.

Exercise F. | Draft 2

Walk around and monitor students as they work. Provide assistance as needed.

Writing Task: Editing

(page 162)

Exercise G. | Editing Practice

- Go over the information in the box.
- Allow time for students to find and correct the mistakes.
- Invite volunteers to write the corrected sentences on the board.

Answer Key

1. Vegetarianism**,** which means not eating meat**,** is one way to reduce greenhouse gases.
2. CFLs, **which** are popular in Japan, use 75 percent less energy than traditional light bulbs.
3. Logging which is done without regulation causes many types of environmental harm.
4. Costa Rica**,** which already generates 80 percent of its energy through renewable sources**,** has promised to have zero net carbon emissions by 2030.

Exercise H. | Editing Checklist

- Read aloud the sentences in the Editing Checklist.
- Allow time for students to read and edit their work.

Exercise I. | Final Draft

- Allow time for students to work on their final draft (or set this for homework).
- Collect their work.

IDEAS FOR . . . Further Research

Ask students to research projects for creating sustainable lifestyles and reducing environmental footprints—for example, ecological farming, ecological homes, recycling, and making products from renewable resources.

Medical Innovators

Academic Track
Health/Medicine

Academic Pathways:
Lesson A: Finding subjects in complex sentences
Making inferences
Lesson B: Understanding an article on technology
Lesson C: Researching information for an essay
Writing a research-based essay

Unit Theme

Unit 8 describes the work of some important medical pioneers as well as some recent developments in medical science.

Think and Discuss *(page 163)*

5 mins

- Ask students to describe the photo. Ask: *What can you see in the photo? Where was this photo taken? What activity is going on here?*
- Discuss question 1 and elicit or name five important medical developments—for example, x-rays, MRIs, vaccines, antibiotics, keyhole surgery.
- Discuss question 2 and elicit or name five serious illnesses that are still without a cure—for example, HIV/AIDS, cancer, malaria, Alzheimer's, Parkinson's.

Exploring the Theme *(pages 164–165)*

15 mins

- The opening spread features a time line showing some of the most important developments in medical history.
- Ask students what the earliest and most recent events on the time line are.
- Ask students to read just the headings and tell you what they know about any of them.
- Discuss question A. Lead a class discussion about why each innovation may have been important.
- Ask students to read the information and write or underline their answers to questions B1–4.
- After checking the answers, ask each group to write five more questions about the text. Then have groups ask each other their questions.

Answer Key

Suggested answers:

A. Answers will vary.
B1. A spiritual problem
2. The basic rules of experimental medicine
3. It made blood transfusions more effective.
4. Answers will vary.

IDEAS FOR . . . Expansion

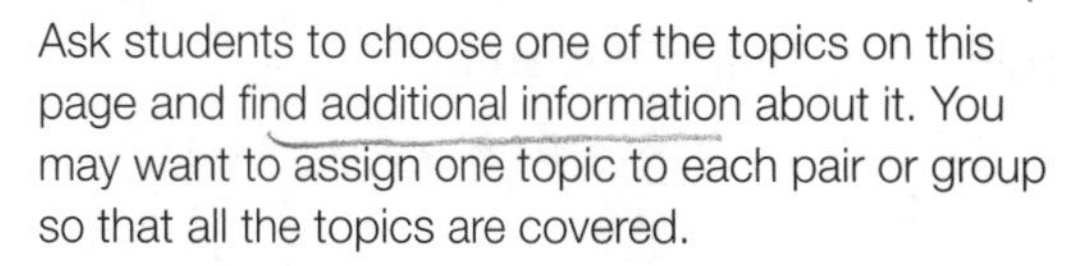

Ask students to choose one of the topics on this page and find additional information about it. You may want to assign one topic to each pair or group so that all the topics are covered.

Discuss medical treatments that are commonly used nowadays and how they help people.

Discuss common illnesses—such as the flu, coughs, migraines, arthritis—and how they are treated. Are these treatments effective? Are they scientifically proven?

Discuss home remedies that are popular in your students' countries. Is there any scientific basis to them?

30 mins

Preparing to Read *(page 166)*

WARM-UP

The Lesson A target vocabulary is presented in the context of a doctor who lived in Andalusia in the tenth century and wrote one of the first manuals of modern medicine.

Ask students what they know about the beginnings of medical science. What kinds of medical methods were used in Europe in the fifteenth and sixteenth centuries?

Exercise A. | Building Vocabulary

- Have students find the words in blue in the reading and use the other words around them to guess their meanings.
- Allow time for students to complete the exercise individually.
- Point out the **Word Link** box. Ask students to use their dictionaries to explain the meanings of these words.
- Tell them to use their dictionaries to find additional words using the prefix *trans-*. (Possible answers: *transcript, transfusion, transform, transmit, transport, transplant)*

Answer Key

1. d **2.** c **3.** g **4.** b **5.** h **6.** f **7.** i **8.** a **9.** e **10.** j

Exercise B. | Using Vocabulary

- Remind students to use the target words in their discussion.
- Compare answers as a class.
- As a follow-up, ask students the following questions: *Who is a* ***pioneer*** *from your country (or from another country)? What did he or she do? What kinds of people need someone to* ***assist*** *them? Who is responsible for* ***compiling*** *a dictionary? Which famous works consist of several* ***volumes****?*

Exercise C. | Brainstorming

- Put students into groups and ask each group to choose one innovator and say what was special about his or her innovation.
- Discuss what students know about changes in medical science over the years.

Answer Key

Possible answers:

1. Answers will vary.
2. Medical knowledge has been passed on by doctors and others who documented their knowledge and experience.

Exercise D. | Predicting

Check the answers after students read the passage.

track 2-05

You may want to play the audio while students read. Remind them that the vocabulary definitions in the footnotes at the bottom of pages 167–169 are intended to help them understand the reading.

Overview of the Reading

The passage describes one of the earliest innovators of modern medicine—a doctor named al-Zahrawi, who developed many new techniques for treating diseases and instruments for performing surgical operations. He also wrote one of the first manuals of modern medicine.

Vocabulary Notes

Ask about or explain the meaning of these additional words in the reading.

healer (title) = someone who cures illnesses
delivery room (paragraph A) = place in a hospital where a woman gives birth
pounding (paragraph A) = beating loudly
physician (paragraph D) = doctor

IDEAS FOR . . . Checking Comprehension

Read out the following details from different paragraphs, and ask students to scan the passage and identify the correct paragraph as quickly as they can.

Which paragraph contains the following information?

1. A type of material for stitching wounds (paragraph F)
2. The date when al-Zahrawi's works were printed (paragraph G)
3. The number of surgical instruments described in his work (paragraph D)
4. The date when he developed the use of forceps (paragraph B)
5. The title of his work (paragraphs D and H)
6. The language in which his work was originally written (paragraph G)
7. The types of surgical instruments described in his work (paragraph F)
8. Where al-Zahrawi worked (paragraph D)

45 mins

Understanding the Reading *(page 170)*

Check students' predictions in exercise **D** on page 166.

Answer Key

The correct answer is a (a medical innovator who lived in Spain many years ago). He did not build a hospital (b) or find a cure for a common disease (c).

Exercise A. | Identifying Main Ideas

- Ask students to read the sentences. Then have them look back at the passage and reread the relevant paragraphs.
- Check the answers and ask students to explain their choices by referring to the text.
- Write the answers on the board.

Answer Key

1. D **2.** E **3.** H **4.** B **5.** G

Exercise B. | Critical Thinking: Making Inferences

- Go over the information in the **CT Focus** box. Point out that inferences are not directly stated by the author; they are conclusions that the reader can draw based on information in the text.
- Ask some questions about the information. Ask: *Which two types of inference are mentioned here? Why are these types of inference important?*
- Explain that question 1 deals with the first type of inference (intended audience) and question 2 deals with the second type of inference (writer's purpose).
- Allow time for students to discuss their answers in pairs before discussing as a class.

Answer Key

1. a (The passage gives a general description of al-Zahrawi's work but does not describe specific medical details.)
2. b (These paragraphs focus on the personal attributes of the doctor, not on the state of medicine at the time.)

Exercise C. | Identifying Key Details

As you check the answers, ask additional questions about each point. For example, for 1–3: *What does the passage tell us about life there? How long ago was he born? What language was it in? What did it contain?*

Answer Key

1. In Andalusia, a region of southern Spain
2. In 936
3. *The Method of Medicine.* It had 30 volumes.
4. Forceps, illustrations of surgical instruments, use of catgut for stitching wounds
5. During an attack on Medina Azahara in 1010
6. The manuscript was secretly passed from person to person, translated into Latin, and then printed.

Exercise D. | Discussing Ideas

- After students have discussed the questions in groups, ask volunteers to summarize the most interesting points for the class. What other questions came up during their discussions?
- Ask these follow-up questions: *How are medical advances made nowadays? What kinds of research and evidence do doctors use to develop their medical knowledge?*

45 mins

Developing Reading Skills
(page 172)

Reading Skill: Finding Subjects in Complex Sentences

- Go over the information in the **Reading Skill** box.
- Ask some questions to check comprehension: *What is a complex sentence? What is a main clause? What is a dependent clause? What is the difference between a main clause and a dependent clause?*
- Ask students to identify which of these conjunctions express purpose (*in order to, so that*), cause (*since, because, as*), condition (*if, even if, unless*), and time sequence (*before, after, when, while*).
- Note that complex sentences can also consist of two main clauses connected by a coordinating conjunction: *and, but, or, yet,* or *so*.
- In the examples given, the main clauses are underlined, while the verbs and their subjects are shown in bold.

Exercise A. | Applying

For extra practice, ask students to identify dependent clauses and conjunctions in these sentences.

Answer Key

1. Her heart is pounding because she fears this is the last time she will see the city.
2. The pain is so strong that she loses consciousness for a few moments.
3. In fact, al-Zahrawi pioneered the use of forceps about 50 years earlier, when he was just starting his medical career.
4. During his decades-long career, he compiled huge amounts of medical knowledge based on existing texts and his own experience.
5. The book also includes the world's first illustrations of surgical instruments—sketches of various surgical hooks, knives, scissors, and forceps—many of which look very familiar today.
6. Although surgery was still dangerous and painful, al-Zahrawi's tools would have helped to treat patients suffering from bone diseases, bladder stones, and wounds.
7. Amazingly, given its importance and influence, *Al-Tasrif* was almost lost forever during an attack on Medina Azahara in 1010.
8. The printed translation enabled al-Zahrawi's innovations and observations to spread throughout Europe, where they had an enormous influence on medicine and surgery.

IDEAS FOR . . . Expansion

Ask students to select another complex sentence from the passage and identify the main clause and the subject. Have students discuss their examples in pairs.

30 mins

Viewing: Healthcare Innovator *(page 173)*

Overview of the Video

The video describes one way that cell phone technology is being used to fight infectious diseases.

Vocabulary Notes

leverage = use something that exists more effectively
component = part
timely = at the right time
platform = a computer operating system
smart application = a type of software designed for a specific task
rapid = fast
insert = put in
menu = list of options or commands
capture = record
valid = correct, accurate
upload = send data from a local computer (or cell phone) to a remote one
server = the main computer in a network
policy maker = person or group that makes decisions about health policy, e.g., funding, distribution of resources
screen = monitor, check

Before Viewing

Exercise A. | Using a Dictionary

- Have students work individually to match the words and their definitions.
- Write the answers on the board.
- Ask students to predict how these words will be used in the video.

Answer Key

1. mitigate **2.** attachment **3.** monitor **4.** diagnose **5.** process **6.** close to

Exercise B. | Thinking Ahead

Discuss the kinds of things that we use cell phones for. Make a list on the board. Which of these could be useful for medical professionals?

Vocabulary Note

An *infectious disease* is one that can be passed on from one person to another—for example, the flu or malaria. Infectious diseases can be caused by bacteria, fungi, or parasites.

While Viewing

Exercise A.

Play the video as students write short answers to the questions.

Exercise B.

Replay the relevant part of the video so that students can number the steps.

After Viewing

Exercise A.

- Have students work in pairs to discuss and compare answers.
- Play the video again if necessary.
- Check the answers.
- Ask students for their opinions of this technology. Do they think it is helpful? What other kinds of diseases could it help with?

Answer Key

A
1. Because they can kill.
2. 70 percent
3. Because it is easy to insert the attachment and process the test immediately. Then the data can be uploaded to an external server.

B
1. Insert the attachment onto the back of the phone.
2. Click on "Malaria."
3. Click on the image of the diagnostic test.
4. Send the result to a central server.

Exercise B. | Critical Thinking: Synthesizing

- Ask students what they admire about this person and what makes him a pioneer in his field.
- Discuss the importance of tracking diseases globally. How can that help healthcare workers and policy makers?

Answer Key

Possible answer:

They are both innovators/pioneers. They want to help people who are ill. They try to develop new technology.

IDEAS FOR . . . Checking Comprehension

Ask these additional questions about the video, or write them on the board.

1. What is new about the technology Aydogan developed? (It's a new way of using cell phones.)
2. What can this new technology do? (It can track, diagnose, and monitor diseases globally. It can process tests rapidly.)
3. How does this help healthcare workers and policy makers? (They can understand the cause-effect relationships of some of the outcomes of different diseases that they are treating.)

IDEAS FOR . . . Expansion

Ask students to research the invention or discovery of one of the following and give a presentation to the class or create a written poster for display in the classroom.

antibiotics	ultrasound
anesthesia	MRI
antiseptic surgery	pacemaker
vaccinations	contact lenses
x-rays	DNA

30 mins

Preparing to Read *(page 174)*

WARM-UP

Lesson B target vocabulary is presented in the context of two recent advances in medical science: regenerative medicine and nanotechnology.

Ask students what types of recent medical advances they know about, for example new drugs, procedures, technologies, or alternative options. Which ones have they heard or read positive things about?

Exercise A. | Building Vocabulary

- Draw students' attention to the **Word Link** box. Ask students to give example sentences for each word.
- Tell students to use their dictionaries to find other words with this root—for example, *collaborative, collaboration, laborious, labor-saving, labor-intensive.*

Answer Key

1. laboratory **2.** seek to **3.** adjacent **4.** sphere **5.** replacement **6.** solution **7.** procedure **8.** transplant **9.** reject **10.** option

Exercise B. | Using Vocabulary

- Ask students to work in pairs.
- Make a list of their ideas on the board.
- Draw students' attention to the **Word Partners** box. Ask students to explain the meaning of each phrase.
- Ask some additional questions using the target words: *What is an example of a solution of a solid substance in liquid?* (Sugar or salt in water) *What kinds of human organs can be transplanted?* (Heart, lungs, kidneys, liver, retina)

Exercise C. | Brainstorming

- Ask pairs or groups to create two idea maps, one for organ transplants and one for cancer treatments.
- Write on the board useful vocabulary that comes up—for example, *side effects, remission, tumor.*

Note: This topic may be a sensitive one for students who have suffered from cancer or who have relatives who have had or are undergoing cancer treatment.

Exercise D. | Predicting

Students will check their answers after they read the passage.

track 2-06

You may want to play the audio while students read.

Overview of the Reading

The reading describes two types of medical technology that have huge potential for human medicine.

Vocabulary Notes

limb (paragraph B) = arm or leg
donated (paragraph D) = given by another person
donor (paragraph D) = someone who gives
donor organ (paragraph D) = organ that has been donated by someone, for example, after they die
immune system (paragraph D) = the body's natural defense against infection
implant (paragraph E) = insert something into someone's body using surgery
side effect (paragraph I) = negative effect of a drug or therapy

Note that more vocabulary from the passage will be studied in exercise **B** on page 179.

IDEAS FOR . . . Checking Comprehension

Ask students these additional discussion questions about the reading.

1. What is your opinion of regenerative medicine? What are its advantages and possible disadvantages? What kinds of tests would you like to see before this becomes a common method used on humans?
2. What is your opinion of nanotechnology in medicine? What are its advantages and possible disadvantages? How could it change medical treatments?

45 mins

Understanding the Reading *(pages 179–180)*

Check the answers to exercise **D** on page 174.

Answer Key

The correct answer is a. The passage does not mention the dangers of medical experiments (c) and mentions the history of medical transplants (b) only briefly in paragraph D.

Exercise A. | Identifying Main Ideas

- Ask students to work individually.
- Call on students to read their answers aloud.

Answer Key

1. Regenerative medicine, nanotechnology
2. donor
3. nanoshells, reconnect
4. cancerous cells/tumors

Exercise B. | Identifying Meaning from Context

- Ask students to work in pairs to locate and discuss the meaning of each word in context.
- Check the answers as a class.

Answer Key

1. improved **2.** uses **3.** is only a small amount
4. to paraphrase **5.** reconnect them

Exercise C. | Understanding Referencing

- Refer students to the information about referencing in Unit 6 on page 123. Remind students that a pronoun can refer back to an *antecedent,* a noun that has been previously mentioned in the passage.
- Ask students to explain how to identify the antecedent. (It has to agree in number and gender, and it has to make sense in context.)

Answer Key

1. donor organs **2.** kidney **3.** doctors
4. silica spheres

Exercise D. | Identifying Supporting Details

- Students can work individually or in pairs.
- As you check the answers, ask students to refer to the paragraph letter and part of the passage that provided the answer.

Answer Key

1. Tissues are grown from a patient's own cells. (paragraph D)
2. He successfully transplanted a laboratory-grown bladder. (paragraph C)
3. They are in short supply. They can be rejected. (paragraph D)
4. A pig's kidney that has been washed with a mild detergent (graphic 4)
5. It has no risks or side effects. (paragraph I)

Exercise E. | Critical Thinking: Making Inferences

Review the information about making inferences on page 170.

Answer Key

1. It is probably intended for a general audience with an interest in medical science. First, because it does not contain too many technical terms, and some are explained in the text, for example, *nanometer* in paragraph G and *nanoshells* in paragraph H. Second, because it explains some basic concepts that would already be familiar to medical professionals—for example, the problems with donor organs in paragraph D.
2. The writer is optimistic about both regenerative medicine and nanotechnology. In paragraph F, "The continuing research of scientists such as these may eventually make donor organs unnecessary and, as a result, significantly increase individuals' chances of survival." In paragraph I, "nanotechnology promises treatment without the risks or side effects."

Exercise F. | Critical Thinking: Synthesizing

Lead a class discussion of the answers.

Answer Key

Possible answers:

1. Nanotechnology could be used to destroy cancerous cells before an organ transplant.
2. They are both pioneers in medical science.
3. They are both ways to stitch parts of the body together.

45 mins

Exploring Written English *(pages 181–182)*

Exercise A. | Brainstorming

- Read the writing goal aloud.
- Brainstorm a few ideas as a class. Suggest some key words to use in an Internet search. Then ask students to continue in pairs.

Writing Skill: Researching Information for an Essay

- Go over the information in the **Writing Skill** box.
- Brainstorm with the class ideas for researching information online—for example, Wikipedia, online journals, online dictionaries, government or educational websites. Ask students to share experiences of using websites for research.
- Ask for some real examples of websites that are reliable and some that are not.
- Ask students to give some examples of websites they use regularly. Have them evaluate the sites using these criteria.
- Explain that you can save time by identifying the websites that are more likely to be reliable.

> **IDEAS FOR . . . Expansion**
>
> To give students practice with researching and comparing different websites, ask them to use the Internet to research a fact such as the date of the first Thanksgiving in the U.S. Ask them to find out how many answers they found and which websites they found to be most reliable.

Exercise B. | Critical Thinking: Evaluating Sources

P. 181

Go over the instructions for this task. Which of these websites would be most appropriate to quote as sources in a class assignment or research paper?

Websites

Answer Key

Possible answers:

a. 4 **b.** 3 **c.** 2 **d.** 1 **e.** 5

Note: Item d is more reliable than c because it is updated weekly. Item e is the least reliable because its purpose is to sell products—not to give a balanced opinion.

TIP Have students create a class list of websites that they use for research and can recommend to classmates. Ask volunteers to compile them as a list and email them to everyone in the class.

Exercise C. | Beginning Your Research

- You may want to brainstorm different areas of medicine, for example, infectious diseases, transplants, prosthetics, cancer diagnosis and treatment, gene therapy, stem cell research. Then assign different areas of medicine to different groups.
- Alternatively, you may want to brainstorm a list of health problems (cancer, HIV, Alzheimer's, Parkinson's, addiction, obesity, etc.). Then have students research the latest medical developments.

Exercise D.

P. 182

- Discuss the difference between a quote and a paraphrase. (A quote uses the person's exact words in quotation marks. A paraphrase summarizes the person's view in different words and doesn't use quotation marks.)
- Refer students back to page 55 in Unit 3 for information they previously studied on quotes and paraphrases.
- Ask students why quotes and paraphrases are necessary. (They provide support for arguments based on research or experience of an independent source and help to make the argument more objective and therefore more convincing.)
- Go over the information in the **Language for Writing** box.
- Refer students to page 249 if necessary.
- When checking the answers, remind students that it is important to state *who* the quote or paraphrase is from—and not just the person's name, but his or her status and credentials as well.

Answer Key

Quote

1. "So I decided to gather consistent information on 19 cities that will have more than 20 million people in the 21st century. [That's what 19.20.21 is about]," says Richard Wurman, an architect and urban planner.
2. Richard Wurman, an architect and urban planner, decided to gather data on 19 cities that will have more than 20 million people in the 21st century.

TIP Remind students that it is important to keep careful records of sources they have consulted (online or print) so that the sources can be referred to in the essay and included in the list of references at the end of the essay. Also remind students that it is not appropriate to include quotes without identifying the source and that plagiarism is severely punished in many colleges and universities.

Writing Task: Drafting

(page 183)

Exercise A. | Planning

- Go over the five steps in this exercise.
- Allow time for students to complete their charts, using ideas from exercise **A** as appropriate.
- Move around the class while students are writing, offering help and advice as needed.
- Ask one or two students to read their thesis statements aloud.

Exercise B. | Draft 1

- As students write their first draft, walk around and offer help as needed.
- You may want to set this task for homework.

Writing Task: Revising

(pages 184–185)

Exercise C. | Critical Thinking: Analyzing

- Explain that analyzing this model essay will help students to revise their own writing.
- Allow time for students to work in pairs.
- Ask students for their opinions about what they liked or disliked in this essay.

Answer Key

1. **Thesis statement:** He and his research team have developed a way to turn regular cell phones into diagnostic tools.
2. **Topic sentences:** 1) Ozcan's invention is important because it is very accurate and easy to use.
   2) Another reason that Ozcan's invention is important is that it is inexpensive.
3. **Answer reader questions:** 1) Doctors do not always have the training to correctly interpret what they see. (What is the problem with existing methods?) 2) His technology only requires a modified cell phone and an Internet connection. (Why is this technology more effective?)
4. **Final Thought:** Ozcan's simple tool might save the lives of millions of people all over the world.

Exercise D. | Revising

Ask students to reread their work carefully and look for ways to improve it.

Exercise E. | Peer Evaluation

- Explain that this process will help students to see if they have organized their ideas clearly.
- Discuss the four steps in the evaluation process to make sure students know what to do.
- Ensure that both members of the pair have equal time to give feedback.

Exercise F. | Draft 2

Walk around and monitor students as they work. Provide assistance as needed.

Writing Task: Editing

(page 186)

Exercise G. | Editing Practice

- Go over the information in the box.
- Allow time for students to find and correct the mistakes.
- Invite volunteers to write the corrected sentences on the board.

Answer Key

1. The article "The Healer of Córdoba" explains that al-Zahrawi was born in Córdoba in **936**.
2. According to the article**,** al-Zahrawi was a physician for the royal court.
3. The article says **that** more than four centuries after they were written, parts of the work were finally printed in 1471.
4. "When income rises, people have money to buy more space**,"** says urban planner Shlomo Angel in the article "Living on an Urban Planet."
5. According to Richard Wurman, an architect and urban planner, "People flock to cities because of the possibilities of doing things that interest them."

Exercise H. | Editing Checklist

- Read aloud the sentences in the Editing Checklist.
- Allow time for students to read and edit their work.

Exercise I. | Final Draft

- Allow time for students to work on their final draft (or set this for homework).
- Collect their work.

IDEAS FOR . . . Further Research

Ask students to research one of these topics for homework and present the results of their research to the class in the next lesson.

- Ancient Greek theories about the causes of illness
- Medical methods in Europe in the 15th and 16th centuries
- Differences between Chinese and Western medicine
- The role of the midwife in the 17th and 18th centuries in Europe and North America
- Native American approaches to healing and medicine

World Languages

Academic Track
Anthropology/Linguistics

Academic Pathways:
Lesson A: Understanding degrees of certainty
Considering counterarguments
Lesson B: Understanding a persuasive text
Lesson C: Using a graphic organizer to plan an essay
Writing an argument essay

Unit Theme

Unit 9 explores the future role of English as a world language and explains why some of the world's smaller languages are in danger of disappearing. It describes the work of some organizations that are trying to preserve disappearing languages.

Think and Discuss *(page 187)*

5 mins

- Ask students to describe the man's gesture and then discuss question 1.
- Discuss other gestures that are used in English and in your students' first language(s). Are there any gestures that have different meanings in different languages?
- Call attention to the photo caption. Discuss what an endangered language is and why a language may disappear.
- Discuss question 2 and make a list of advantages on the board. For example, you can understand and learn about other cultures, communicate with people from other countries, have better job and career opportunities, and it keeps your brain active.

Exploring the Theme *(pages 188–189)*

15 mins

- The opening spread features a world map showing the distribution of the major language families.
- Survey the class to find out how many languages are spoken (or have been/are being studied) by students in your class.
- Discuss the map. What do the colors mean? What are the differences between these language families?
- Ask students to choose two languages from different families and say how they are different. Then ask students to choose two languages from one of the major families and say how they are similar and different.
- Discuss question A1. Get students' thoughts on why Indo-European languages are so widespread.
- Discuss question A2. It may help to look at a physical map of the world to answer this question.
- Point out the two charts. Ask students to describe what is shown in each one.
- In the first chart (page 188), what does the color red represent? What do the squares represent?
- In the second chart (on page 189), what does the color green signify? What does the red line represent?
- Discuss questions B1–2.

Answer Key

Possible answers:

A1. Indo-European. Europe, North America, South America, Australia
2. They are probably unrelated to the major language families.
B1–2. Answers will vary.

IDEAS FOR . . . Expansion

Ask students to research the development of the English language and find out how it became established as a dominant language in the world.

30 mins

Preparing to Read *(page 190)*

WARM-UP

The Lesson A target vocabulary is presented in the context of the role of English and other languages in the future.

Ask students what they think about English as a world language. Do they think it is the most useful language? What are its advantages and disadvantages? Do they think any other languages would be more suitable?

Exercise A. | Building Vocabulary

- Have students find the words in blue in the reading and use the other words around them to guess their meanings.
- Allow time for students to complete the exercise individually.
- Check the answers and ask for other word forms of these words—for example, *constitution, facilitator, acquisition, prominence, anticipation.*
- Point out the **Word Link** box. Ask students to use their dictionaries to explain the meanings of these words.
- Tell them to find the meaning of these additional words using the root *lingu-: neurolinguistics, sociolinguistics, paralinguistics, audiolingual.*

Answer Key

1. linguistic	**6.** furthermore
2. facilitate	**7.** constitute
3. anticipate	**8.** switch
4. prominent	**9.** considerably
5. acquire	**10.** scale

Exercise B. | Using Vocabulary

- Remind students to use the target words in their discussion.
- Encourage class discussion of questions 1 and 2, as a wide variety of answers are possible.

Vocabulary Note

For question 2, you may want to distinguish between *acquiring* a language (learning it as your first language) and *learning* a language (studying it later after acquiring your first language).

Answer Key

Possible answers:

1. People who are bilingual; people who live in a country where two languages are spoken; people who live in a foreign country and speak one language at home and a different one at school and/or work
2. To live in or visit the country where it is spoken; to learn the language as a child
3. Answers will vary.

Exercise C. | Brainstorming

When students have finished discussing the questions, ask a spokesperson from each group to report to the class the main points of their discussion.

Exercise D. | Predicting

Check the answers after students read the entire passage.

track 2-07

You may want to play the audio while students read. Remind them that the vocabulary definitions in the footnotes at the bottom of pages 191–193 will help them understand the reading.

Overview of the Reading

The passage describes the conclusions of a study carried out by David Graddol, a researcher on the future of language. He concludes that the role of English as a global language is changing and that in the future it will become common for people to speak many languages, not just English.

Vocabulary Notes

Ask about or explain the meaning of these additional words in the reading.

native speaker (paragraph B) = person who speaks the language as his or her first language
journal literature (paragraph E) = academic or scientific articles in academic journals
competence (paragraph F) = knowledge or ability
predominance (paragraph F) = being the strongest or most powerful
find oneself (or *be*) *at a disadvantage* (paragraph F) = be less successful
dominant (paragraph G) = important, powerful
Note that some additional vocabulary from the reading will be studied in exercise **C** on page 195.

IDEAS FOR . . . Checking Comprehension

Ask students to paraphrase the following sentences in their own words.

1. A new linguistic order is about to emerge. (paragraph A)
2. Mandarin Chinese will probably be the next must-learn language. (paragraph C)
3. Businesses whose employees speak only one language will find themselves at a disadvantage. (paragraph F)
4. Some monolingual speakers, especially native English speakers . . . have been too complacent about . . . the lack of need to learn other languages. (paragraph G)

Discuss the following questions with the class.

1. How would you feel about learning Mandarin Chinese (or Spanish or Arabic) instead of English?
2. How would you feel about learning several languages, not just one?
3. What kind of language was Latin, and why did it dominate Europe?

45 mins

Understanding the Reading

(pages 194–195)

Check students' predictions in exercise **D** on page 190.

Answer Key

The correct answer is a (the role of English and other languages in the future).

Exercise A. | Identifying Main Ideas

- Ask students to read the sentences. Then have them look back at the passage and reread the relevant paragraphs.
- Check the answers and ask students to explain their choices by referring to the text.
- Write the answers on the board.

Answer Key

1. G **2.** D **3.** A **4.** F **5.** C **6.** B **7.** E

Exercise B. | Scanning for Key Details

- Ask students to complete their answers individually and then compare with a partner.
- Check the answers and ask which paragraph contained the relevant information.

Answer Key

1. in developing countries (paragraph A)
2. Bengali, Tamil, and Malay (paragraph B)
3. It allows for greater international collaboration and research. (paragraph E)
4. more than 90 percent (paragraph E)
5. Latin. It was dominant in Europe until the end of the 1600s. (paragraph G)
6. Because they are official languages in more than half (100) of the countries in the world and they are the first or second language of 2.8 billion people on the planet, about 40 percent of the world's population. (paragraph H)

Exercise C. | Identifying Meaning from Context

- Allow time for students to reread the relevant parts of the passage and figure out the answers.
- Check the answers as a class.
- Ask students to make up other example sentences using these words or to look them up in the dictionary to find other possible meanings.

Answer Key

1. a **2.** a **3.** b **4.** a

Exercise D. | Interpreting Visual Information

- Discuss the two graphics (a word cloud and a bar graph) on page 192, and ask students to describe them and say what they represent.
- Ask if students were surprised by any data shown there. What questions could they ask about these graphics?
- Discuss which countries use Chinese and Spanish as their main language. How similar are the different varieties of Chinese and Spanish to each other?

Answer Key

1. The size of the word represents the number of speakers.
2. Chinese, Spanish
3. There are more English speakers than Chinese speakers in the word cloud. The word cloud includes non-native speakers of English.

Exercise E. | Critical Thinking: Personalizing

Use the answers to these questions to lead into a general discussion of reasons for learning English or another language.

45 mins

Developing Reading Skills

(page 196)

Reading Skill: Understanding Degrees of Certainty

- Go over the information in the **Reading Skill** box.
- Ask some questions to check comprehension: *Which modal expresses certainty?* (will) *Which modals express uncertainty?* (may, might, could) *Which expresses more certainty:* we anticipate that *or* it is likely that?

> **IDEAS FOR . . . Presenting Grammar**
>
> Read some sentences from the passage, and ask students to rephrase them using one of the expressions from the box.
>
> For example:
> T: The number of native English speakers is decreasing.
> S: The number of native English speakers may decrease.
> S: It is (or It seems) likely that the number of native English speakers will decrease.
> S: Some experts anticipate that the number of native English speakers will decrease.

Exercise A. | Critical Thinking: Inferring Degrees of Certainty

Give one or two examples (see possible answers). Then allow time for students to work in pairs and study the passage.

> **Answer Key**
>
> Possible answers: 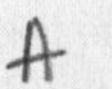
>
> 1. Paragraph B: By 2050, the number (of people who speak English as a first language) is expected to be just five percent. (certain)
>   Paragraph C: It seems likely that no one language will dominate in the near future. (less certain)
> 2. Answers will vary.

Exercise B. | Applying

- Remind students to use a variety of modals and other expressions in their discussions.
- Ask students to choose one of these questions and explain their opinion to the class. Alternatively, they can write their opinion as a journal entry.

> **IDEAS FOR . . . Expansion**
>
> Ask students to make a prediction about the future of English (using one of the expressions from the **Reading Skill** box) and write it on a slip of paper. Collect the papers and redistribute them. Ask pairs of students to discuss their new sentences. Finally, ask each pair to read their sentences aloud and give their opinion about each sentence's likelihood, giving reasons for their opinion.

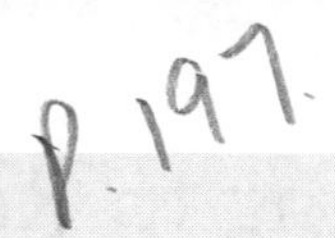

30 mins

Viewing: Enduring Voices

(page 197)

Overview of the Video

The video presents information about a project aimed at bringing awareness to disappearing languages.

Before Viewing

Exercise A. | Using a Dictionary

- Ask a volunteer to read the paragraph aloud.
- Have students work individually to match the words and their definitions.
- Write the answers on the board.
- Ask some general questions about the text: *What is the Living Tongues Institute? Why were younger people neglecting their parents' language? What were they losing?*

Answer Key

1. vital **2.** heritage **3.** die out **4.** shift over to **5.** neglecting

Exercise B. | Thinking Ahead

After students discuss the question in pairs, gather ideas from the class and write them on the board in the form of an idea map.

While Viewing

Play the video while students write short answers to the questions.

After Viewing

Exercise A.

- Have students work in pairs to discuss and compare answers.
- Play the video again if necessary.
- Check the answers.
- Lead a class discussion on why it is important to preserve languages.

Answer Key

1. They are trying to preserve dying languages so that words, ideas, and valuable information will not be lost forever.
2. Because they are the last speakers of the language and when they die, the language will die, too.
3. They document the language and also train local people to use special language technology kits to help communities document the last speakers of old languages.
4. They hope the kits will help inspire younger people to take an interest in the words of their elders, perhaps encouraging them to keep a language alive by speaking it themselves.

Exercise B. | Synthesizing

Ask students how they feel about this project. Are there any languages in their countries that are endangered?

Answer Key

Possible answers:

Because they can use English to get a better education and a better job and speak with people from other countries.

IDEAS FOR . . . Checking Comprehension

Ask these additional questions about the video, or write them on the board.

1. Where is the village of Hong? (In the extreme northeast of India, a remote area bordering Bhutan, Myanmar, and China)
2. What are some of the problems with recording dying languages? (They are not written down. The speakers are very old, and they may not remember everything.)
3. What is in the language technology kit? (A laptop computer, digital cameras, and digital recorders)
4. What kinds of ideas do you think might get lost when a language disappears? (Answers will vary.)

IDEAS FOR . . . Expansion

Ask students to find out more about the Living Tongues Institute for homework.

More information about it can be found here: http://www.livingtongues.org/

Preparing to Read *(page 198)*

30 mins

WARM-UP

Lesson B target vocabulary is presented in the context of languages that are in danger of disappearing and various organizations that are working to preserve them.

Ask students what they know about endangered languages. Why do they think some languages might be in danger of disappearing? What languages do they know of that are no longer spoken?

Exercise A. | Building Vocabulary

- Ask students which of these words they are already familiar with and in what contexts they have seen and/or heard them.
- After checking the answers, tell students to use their dictionaries to find other word forms of these words—for example, *accuracy, categorize, conformity, deprivation.*

Answer Key

1. portion	**6.** institution
2. assign	**7.** deprive
3. critically	**8.** accurately
4. category	**9.** attitude
5. maintain	**10.** conform

Exercise B. | Using Vocabulary

- Ask students to work in pairs.
- Ask each pair to present one idea for each question to the class. Use students' ideas to make a list on the board.
- Draw students' attention to the **Word Partners** box. Ask students to explain the meaning of each phrase.
- Ask some additional questions using the target words from exercise **A:** *What kinds of pressures are there to* ***conform*** *in society? What factors can* ***deprive*** *people of opportunities? What can help you to* ***maintain*** *motivation when learning a language?*

Exercise C. | Predicting

Students will check their answers after reading the entire passage.

track 2-08

You may want to play the audio while students read. Remind them that the vocabulary definitions in the footnotes at the bottom of pages 200–202 will help them understand the reading.

Overview of the Reading

The reading explains why many smaller languages are disappearing and gives some examples of their unique characteristics. It also describes different ways in which some organizations are trying to preserve endangered languages.

Vocabulary Notes

remote (paragraph D) = distant, difficult to reach
spectrum (paragraph E) = range of colors
nutritional (paragraph F) = healthy
invaluable (paragraph G) = precious, useful
encoded (paragraph G) = carrying information
hot spot (paragraph H) = place of crisis or danger
a wealth of (knowledge, experience, etc.) (paragraph I) = a large amount of

Note that more vocabulary from the passage will be studied in exercise **B** on page 203.

IDEAS FOR . . . Checking Comprehension

Ask students these additional questions about the reading, or write them on the board.

1. How does each of the following concepts differ in the languages mentioned in the reading: 1) time 2) number 3) color 4) family relationships?
2. How do these organizations record data of disappearing languages and prevent them from vanishing?

Understanding the Reading *(pages 203–204)*

45 mins

Check the answers to exercise **C** on page 198.

Answer Key

The correct answer is c (how languages disappear and ways to keep them alive). The passage does not give details about languages in North America and Australia (b). It mentions a few examples of unique features of some languages (a), but they are not the main focus of the passage.

Exercise A. | Identifying Main Ideas

- Ask students to work individually.
- Call on students to read their answers aloud.

Answer Key

1. distribution
2. smaller, extinction/dying out/disappearing
3. values, history, traditions, institutions, unique experiences
4. knowledge of plants and animals
5. to preserve disappearing languages

Exercise B. | Identifying Meaning from Context

- Ask students to work in pairs to locate and discuss the meaning of each word in context.
- Check the answers as a class.
- Ask students to make up additional sentences that illustrate the meaning of each word or phrase.

Answer Key

1. b **2.** b **3.** a **4.** a

Exercise C. | Interpreting Visual Information

- Discuss the map as a class. Name the continents. Name the different colors. (Dark red, orange, yellow or ochre, and olive green). Ask: *What do the regions with languages at highest risk have in common?*
- Discuss the questions as a class.
- Ask students to describe the map in their own words. For example: *The map shows . . ., The colors represent . . ., The information tells us that . . .*

P200

- You may want to ask students to write a description of the map for homework.

Answer Key

1. It shows places where languages are at risk of extinction. They show the degree of risk.
2. Central and Eastern Siberia, Northern Australia, Northwest Pacific Plateau, Central South America
3. It shows where organizations such as Enduring Voices need to target their efforts.

Exercise D. | Identifying Supporting Details

- Students can work individually or in pairs.
- As you check the answers, ask students to refer to the paragraph letter and part of the passage that provided the answer.

Answer Key

1. Tuvan, Aka, Seri, Djawi
2. more than 1,000
3. They are taken over by more dominant languages, political pressures, commercial pressures.
4. They use relative words such as *few* and *many*. This tells us that the concept of assigning numbers may be culturally relative, not innate.
5. It can tell them information about plants and animals. We can learn other important scientific information.
6. The goal is to preserve disappearing languages. They document and record the cultural information the languages contain.

Exercise E. | Critical Thinking: Understanding Predictions

- Review the information about degrees of certainty on page 196.
- Discuss the answers as a class.

Answer Key

1–2. That within the next century, nearly half of the world's current languages may disappear. (paragraph B)

The disappearance of the (Seri) language might therefore deprive us of important scientific knowledge. (paragraph F)

We may lose knowledge about plants that could someday lead to an invaluable medicine, not to mention information about the history and survival skills of many of the world's cultures. (paragraph G)

Their efforts and the work of other language preservationists will allow us to pass on a wealth of historical, cultural, and scientific knowledge to future generations. (paragraph I)

3. He feels more certain about the last prediction and less certain about the others.

Exercise F. | Critical Thinking: Considering Counterarguments

- Go over the information in the **CT Focus** box.
- Ask students to identify the arguments in favor of saving endangered languages that are mentioned in the reading. Are any counterarguments mentioned?
- Ask students to discuss the questions in groups and make a list of counterarguments.
- If time is available, have them role-play a debate between someone in favor of and someone against the saving of endangered languages.

45 mins

Exploring Written English *(pages 205–206)*

Exercise A. | Brainstorming

- Read the writing goal aloud.
- Explain the purpose of a persuasive essay, and contrast this with other types of essays such as descriptive or comparison.
- Brainstorm a few ideas as a class.

Writing Skill: Using a Graphic Organizer to Plan an Essay

- Ask students for examples of different types of graphic organizers (for example, a Venn diagram, a mind map, a pie chart).
- Ask students why it is useful to use a graphic organizer. (It helps you to develop and organize ideas before you start writing.)
- Go over the information in the **Writing Skill** box.
- Ask volunteers to read out the information in the T-chart. Can they add any more ideas?

> **IDEAS FOR . . . Expansion**
>
> To give students practice with researching and comparing different websites, ask them to use the Internet to research a fact such as how many languages are spoken in South Africa. Ask them to share with the class how many answers they found and which websites they found to be most reliable.

Exercise B. | Using a T-chart

- Allow time for students to work individually. Then have them compare ideas in pairs.
- Draw a T-chart on the board and invite volunteers to come to the board to write their ideas.
- Take a class vote on who agrees with which side of the argument.
- Allow five minutes for students to free write about the opposing point of view.

Answer Key

Possible answers:

Pro:
Promote intercultural understanding
More efficient use of resources
Less need for translators and interpreters

Con:
Lose valuable cultural heritage/history
Become less creative
Less variety in culture and literature

Exercise C. | Doing Research

- You may want to brainstorm key words that students can use in their research.
- Remind students to keep notes of all sources to use in their references later.

Exercise D.

- Go over the information in the **Language for Writing** box.
- Point out that each of these sentences consists of two clauses separated by a comma. The clause introduced by *while* (or *even though* or *although*) presents the information that is less important.
- Explain that combining information in this way helps to make the argument more persuasive.

Answer Key

Possible answers:

1. Argument: Although Mandarin is difficult to learn, it could be useful in the world of business.
2. Argument: While language diversity may lead to misunderstanding or conflict, we must preserve smaller languages because of the important knowledge they contain.

Exercise E.

- Monitor students as they write, and pinpoint any trouble spots.
- Ask volunteers to read their sentences aloud.

TIP It may be helpful to have students refer back to previous essays (for example, the persuasive essay in Unit 7) and identify places where they could introduce a counterargument using *while*.

Writing Task: Drafting

(page 207)

Exercise A. | Planning

- Go over the five steps in this exercise.
- Allow time for students to complete their charts, using ideas from exercises **A** and **B** as appropriate.
- Move around the class while students are writing, offering help and advice as needed.
- Ask one or two students to read out their thesis statements.

Exercise B. | Draft 1

- As students write their first draft, walk around and offer help as needed.
- You may want to set this task for homework.

Writing Task: Revising

(pages 208–209)

Exercise C. | Critical Thinking: Analyzing

- Explain that analyzing this model essay will help students to revise their own writing.
- Allow time for students to work in pairs.
- Ask students to identify the counterarguments and evaluate the use of sources.
- Ask students what they liked or disliked in this essay. What points did they find most convincing and why?

Answer Key

1. **Thesis statement:** Corporations should not pay for their employees to learn a second language because it is expensive, some people may not have the ability to learn another language, and the process is far too time-consuming.
2. **Three arguments:** expensive, some people may not have the ability to learn another language, time-consuming.
3. **Topic sentences:** 1) Sending employees to language schools is expensive. 2) Another reason companies should not pay for their employees to learn a second language is that some people may not be capable of learning an extra language. 3) Finally, language learning is far too time-consuming.
4. **Key Words:** 1) expensive 2) some people may not be capable of learning an extra language 3) time-consuming
5. **Counterarguments:**
   (paragraph 2) While some people may think that they can save money by learning on their own using self-study websites or CD-ROM programs, most experts agree that effective language learning only takes place in a classroom with a qualified teacher.

   (paragraph 3) While it may be possible to become fluent in a second language at any age, many experts believe that age is still an important factor.

   (paragraph 4) Even though some language programs promise fluency in a short period of time, the average language learner needs constant and long-term exposure to a second language in order to become even somewhat fluent.

   Sources:
   (paragraph 2) However, the cost of classroom instruction adds up over time. For example, according to the *New York Times* article "Foreign Language Courses, Brushing Up or Immersion," the cost of classroom instruction in the United States can range from $480 to $590 for an average three-month course.

   (paragraph 3) According to the website for the Center for Advanced Research on Language Acquisition, research shows that people's ability to learn a foreign language deteriorates as they age.

   (paragraph 4) For example, according to the online article "How Long Does It Take to Learn a New Language?," a typical employee taking two hours off work each day to study a language would take several years to become even relatively fluent.

Exercise D. | Revising

Ask students to reread their work carefully and look for ways to improve it.

Exercise E. | Peer Evaluation

- Explain that this process will help students to see if they have organized their ideas clearly.
- Discuss the four steps in the evaluation process to make sure students know what to do.
- Ensure that both members of the pair have equal time to give feedback.

Exercise F. | Draft 2

Walk around and monitor students as they work. Provide assistance as needed.

Writing Task: Editing

(page 210)

Exercise G. | Editing Practice

- Go over the information in the box.
- Allow time for students to find and correct the mistakes.
- Invite volunteers to write the corrected sentences on the board.

Answer Key

1. While language instruction may **be** expensive, it is important that children learn a second language in order to compete in the global economy.
2. Even though Mandarin may soon become an important world language, **it** probably won't be the dominant language because the writing system is too difficult.
3. Although French may have been a diplomatic language in the past**,** it shouldn't be an official UN language because there are too few native French speakers.
4. While children **must learn** the dominant language of their region in order to succeed in school and in business, they should also preserve their native languages in order to retain culture and history.

Exercise H. | Editing Checklist

- Read aloud the sentences in the Editing Checklist.
- Allow time for students to read and edit their work.

Exercise I. | Final Draft

- Allow time for students to work on their final draft (or set this for homework).
- Collect their work.

IDEAS FOR . . . Further Research

Ask students to write about one of the following.

- Differences between their language and English and how this can cause problems for learning English
- Concepts that exist in their language but not in English (and vice versa) and what this says about these two cultures
- Research into English as a *lingua franca*. How is it different from English spoken in the U.S. or the U.K.?
- Differences between English spoken in the U.K, the U.S., Canada, and Australia

Survival Instinct

Academic Track
Psychology

Academic Pathways:

Lesson A: Identifying adverbial phrases
Inferring the purpose of stories and anecdotes

Lesson B: Understanding a factual text and a personal narrative

Lesson C: Planning and writing a descriptive narrative

Unit Theme

Unit 10 explores the physical symptoms of fear and how we can use our brain to control our fear and survive life-threatening situations.

Think and Discuss *(page 211)*

5 mins

- Ask students what they understand from the unit title.
- Ask students to describe the photo. What could have caused this crash? (Engine failure, systems malfunction, poor weather conditions, poor visibility, human error)
- Discuss the questions as a class.
- Discuss any real-life survival stories in the news recently.

TIP **Bring in some local and national newspapers. Give one to each group and have students search them for survival stories. Ask each group to summarize a story for the class.**

Exploring the Theme *(pages 212–213)*

15 mins

- The opening spread features a photo of people on a roller coaster in an amusement park.
- Discuss the photo. Ask: *Why do people enjoy this kind of ride? Would you go on a roller coaster? Why or why not? Has anyone been on a roller coaster? What did you feel?*
- Discuss questions A1–2. Make a list of extreme activities that people enjoy—for example, white-water rafting, ice climbing, shark cage diving.
- Ask students to read the information. Discuss questions B1–2. Discuss in what situations this kind of research could be helpful.

Answer Key

A1. and **2.** Answers will vary.
B1. It means that the fear is closely related to an early stage of human evolution.
B2. They are learning how to help people prepare for dangerous situations.

IDEAS FOR . . . Expansion

Ask students to role-play a debate. Student A wants to ban extreme activities because they are dangerous. Student B thinks they are fun and people should be allowed to do them. Each pair can present a summary of their arguments to the class.

Ask students to choose one extreme activity and find out where it is done, what is dangerous about it, how risky it is, and why people enjoy it.

Discuss why some people enjoy watching horror movies or reading horror stories about zombies, vampires, etc.

30 mins

Preparing to Read *(page 214)*

WARM-UP

The Lesson A target vocabulary is presented in the context of the physical symptoms of fear and how they operate.

Ask students what scares them the most. Spiders? Snakes? Mice? How do they feel when they see something they are afraid of? Ask them to describe their physical and emotional reactions in as much detail as possible.

Note: Keep in mind that the topic of fear in this lesson may be a sensitive one for those students who have experienced life-threatening situations. This may be avoided by keeping the discussion away from specific incidents and focusing on things in general that cause fear. The topic of ghosts or the supernatural may also be sensitive for religious or cultural reasons.

Exercise A. | Building Vocabulary

- Have students find the words in blue in the reading and use the other words around them to guess their meanings.
- Allow time for students to complete the exercise individually.
- Check the answers and ask for other word forms of these words—for example, *advice, react, assumption, secure, priority.*
- Point out the **Word Partners** box. Ask students to use their dictionaries to explain the meanings of these phrases.

Answer Key

1. mode	**6.** incident
2. reaction	**7.** advise
3. assume	**8.** security
4. derived	**9.** trigger
5. prioritize	**10.** distortion

Exercise B. | Using Vocabulary

- Remind students to use the target words in their discussion.
- Call on volunteers to report their answers to the class.
- Ask some additional questions using the target words from exercise **A**: *How do you* ***prioritize*** *things you do every day? Give an example of how the media can give a* ***distortion*** *of reality.*

Exercise C. | Brainstorming

When students have finished discussing the questions, take a class vote on the most common reactions for each situation.

IDEAS FOR . . . Expansion

This may be a good opportunity to teach some adjectives and idioms for expressing fear (see below). Then have students describe seeing something they are afraid of (for example, a spider, a snake) using as many of these idioms as they can.

Adjectives:
anxious, scared, afraid, frightened, terrified, petrified, panic-stricken

Idioms:
My hair stood on end.
I was frozen with fear.
I had my heart in my mouth.
It made my blood run cold.
I had butterflies in my stomach.
I was shaking like a leaf.
I nearly jumped out of my skin.

Exercise D. | Predicting

Check the answers after students read the passage.

track 2-09

You may want to play the audio while students read. Remind them that the vocabulary definitions in the footnotes at the bottom of pages 215–217 will help them understand the reading.

Overview of the Reading

The passage describes our physical reaction to fear in crisis situations. It describes the experience of a man who was taken hostage by armed rebels and his reaction of fear during this incident.

Vocabulary Notes

Ask about or explain the meaning of these additional words in the reading.

host (paragraph A) = person who invites people to a party or other event
hostage (paragraph B) = someone who has been captured and held prisoner in exchange for money or other demands
confess (paragraph C) = admit
shot up (paragraph E) = rose dramatically
detect (paragraph F) = notice
bumper sticker (paragraph F) = a small sign on the back (bumper) of a car that often has a political or humorous message
primal (paragraph G) = primitive, relating to an early stage of human evolution

impair (paragraph J) = weaken or damage
stunned (paragraph J) = amazed

Note that some additional vocabulary from the reading will be studied in exercise C on page 219.

IDEAS FOR . . . Checking Comprehension

Ask students these additional questions about the passage, or write them on the board.

1. What do the two situations in paragraph F illustrate? (That time slowed down and the people were able to notice tiny details)
2. Explain the difference between our immediate reaction and our follow-up reaction to fear. (The first is a signal from the ear to the amygdala. The second is a more detailed but slower signal through the cortex to the amygdala.)
3. How does stress impair the brain's higher-order functions? Give two examples from the passage. (Paragraph B: The ambassador was frozen on the staircase. Paragraph J: Pabon thought his reflection was another man.)

45 mins

Understanding the Reading *(pages 218–219)*

Check students' predictions in exercise **D** on page 214.

Answer Key

The reading passage is about the physical symptoms of fear and how they operate.

Exercise A. | Identifying Main Ideas

- Ask students to read the sentences. Then have them look back at the passage and reread the relevant paragraphs.
- Check the answers and ask students to explain their choices by referring to the text.
- Write the answers on the board.

Answer Key

1. G **2.** E **3.** C **4.** F **5.** D

Exercise B. | Identifying Key Details

- Ask students to complete their answers individually and then compare with a partner.
- Check the answers and ask which paragraph contained the relevant information.

Answer Key

1. He was in the Embassy of the Dominican Republic in Bogotá, Colombia, for a Dominican Independence Day celebration.
2. They were members of M-19, a group of violent nationalist rebels.
3. His blood vessels thinned so that he would bleed less if he were wounded. At the same time, the chemistry of his blood changed so that it could coagulate, or clot, more easily in the case of injury.
4. Cortisol and adrenaline flooded through his body, making his muscles stronger.
5. *Tachypsychia* describes the experience of time slowing down.
6. The upsides are that our bodies become stronger and create their own natural painkillers, and some people experience improved vision. The downside is that we suddenly have trouble solving problems. In a crisis situation, reason-based functions are weaker and slower than the primal, emotional response of the amygdala.
7. Asencio advises us to "concentrate on your thought processes and your plans." By forcing ourselves to think through the problem, to remain calm, to breathe evenly, we may have a greater chance of surviving a life-threatening experience.

Exercise C. | Identifying Meaning from Context

- Allow time for students to reread the relevant parts of the passage and figure out the answers.
- Check the answers as a class.
- Ask students to make up other example sentences using these words or to look them up in the dictionary to find other possible meanings or contexts where they are used.

Answer Key

1. is anxious and excited, not calm
2. not smoothly connected
3. is endless
4. the brain

Exercise D. | Critical Thinking: Analyzing and Inferring Purpose

- Go over the information in the **CT Focus** box.
- Tell a personal anecdote about a time you were afraid. Ask students what aspect of the theory outlined in the reading passage it illustrates.
- Allow time for students to work in pairs to complete the diagram, referring back to the reading passage as they work.
- Draw the diagram on the board and ask students to tell you what to write in each section.

- Discuss which different aspects of the theory these stories illustrate.
- Have students work in pairs to tell a story about a time when they were frightened. Encourage students to discuss what aspect of the theory each story illustrates.

Answer Key

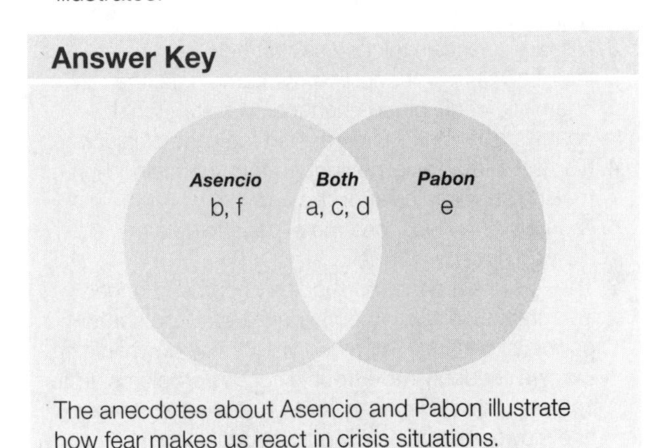

The anecdotes about Asencio and Pabon illustrate how fear makes us react in crisis situations.

45 mins

Developing Reading Skills

(page 220)

Reading Skill: Identifying Adverbial Phrases

- Go over the information in the **Reading Skill** box.
- Explain or elicit the difference between an adverb and an adverbial phrase. Ask some questions to check comprehension: *What do adverbial phrases tell us? How are adverbial phases different from clauses? Give some examples of adverbial phrases that answer the questions* when, why, *or* how.

Exercise A. | Applying, and B. | Critical Thinking: Identifying Purpose

- Do the first item together with the class as an example.
- Check answers as a class.

Answer Key

1. Through his story and those of others who have survived life-threatening situations, (how)
2. After meeting everyone that he had intended to speak with, (when)
3. Just then, (when)
4. silently watching the world collapse around them. (how)
5. As the firing continued, (when)
6. giving his muscles a sudden rush of energy. (how)
7. in life-or-death situations (when)
8. In life-or-death situations, (when)
9. By forcing ourselves to think through the problem, (how)
10. to protect himself. (why)

- When checking the answers to exercise **A**, ask whether each adverbial phrase tells us *when, why,* or *how.*

30 mins

Viewing: Survival Lessons *(page 221)*

Overview of the Video

The video describes ways to respond to shark and elephant attacks that can help you survive.

Before Viewing

Exercise A. | Using a Dictionary

- Have students work individually to match the words and their definitions.
- Write the answers on the board.

Answer Key

1. stealthy **2.** alarmed **3.** stand your ground **4.** charge **5.** tuck in **6.** splash

Exercise B. | Thinking Ahead

- Ask students to explain the reasons for their choices.
- Take a vote on each answer and write the totals on the board.
- Do not check the answers yet. Students will find the answers by watching the video.

Answer Key

1. b **2.** c

While Viewing

Play the video while students write short answers to the questions.

After Viewing

Exercise A.

- As a class, discuss the answers to the exercise **B** Thinking Ahead questions. Were most people in the class right, or not?
- Have students work in pairs to discuss and compare answers to the While Viewing questions.
- Play the video again if necessary.
- Check the answers.
- Discuss what you and the class found most surprising about the information in the video.

Answer Key

1. Less than a hundred
2. Hunger and curiosity
3. It flares its ears and trumpets a warning.

Exercise B. | Critical Thinking: Synthesizing

Ask a spokesperson from each group to report to the class.

IDEAS FOR . . . Checking Comprehension

Ask these additional questions about the video, or write them on the board.

Are these statements true (T) or false (F)? Correct the false statements.

1. There are 300 species of shark. (T)
2. Most species of shark are man-eaters. (F—only a small number are man-eaters)
3. A shark bite is usually deadly. (T)
4. Sharks bite because they are hungry. (F—more often than not it's because they are curious)
5. The shark may swim away if you hit it between its eyes. (T)
6. The elephant weighs five tons. (F—three tons)
7. After shouting, you should run as fast as you can. (F—don't turn your back, stand your ground and shout louder)
8. Elephants can run very fast. (T)

IDEAS FOR . . . Expansion

Ask students to find out more about how to avoid being attacked by wild animals (for example, grizzly bears, tigers, wolves, alligators, snakes, scorpions) and what to do when attacked by one of them.

30 mins

Preparing to Read *(page 222)*

WARM-UP

Lesson B target vocabulary is presented in the context of how breathing and meditation can be used to control our fear in a crisis situation.

Ask students if they have any experience with yoga or meditation or what they know about it.

Exercise A. | Building Vocabulary

- Ask students which of these words they are already familiar with and in what contexts they have seen and/ or heard them.
- After checking the answers, tell students to use their dictionaries to find other word forms of these words—for example, *adverse, consciousness, meditate, mortal, alteration, radicalize, residence, tactic, trauma.*

Answer Key

1. h **2.** b **3.** g **4.** i **5.** d **6.** c **7.** j **8.** a **9.** f **10.** e

Exercise B. | Using Vocabulary

- Ask students to work in pairs.
- Ask each pair to present one idea for each question to the class. Then use students' ideas to make a list on the board.
- Draw students' attention to the **Word Link** box. Ask students to use their dictionaries and try to explain the meanings of these words.
- Ask students to find other words using the root *sci*—for example, *omniscient, prescient, scientific.*
- Ask some additional questions using the target words from exercise **A:** *What kinds of activities require a* ***tactical*** *plan? How many places have you* ***resided*** *in over the last five years? How can you help someone after a* ***traumatic*** *experience?*

Exercise C. | Brainstorming

Compare answers as a class and make a list on the board. (Possible answers: try deep breathing, visualize being calm, talk to a friend)

Exercise D. | Skimming/Predicting

Make sure everyone writes their answers, but don't check them yet. They will be checked after students read the passage in more detail.

track 2-10

You may want to play the audio while students read. Remind them that the vocabulary definitions in the footnotes at the bottom of pages 223–225 will help them understand the reading.

Overview of the Reading

The reading explains how meditation can enable people to use breathing and meditation to control their fear. It describes the experience of a woman who suffered a near-fatal bus accident and was able to control her fear by breathing slowly so that she could escape and get help.

Vocabulary Notes

combat trainer (paragraph B) = military instructor who trains soldiers for combat
FBI (paragraph B) = Federal Bureau of Investigation (federal police department in the U.S.)
slam (paragraph G) = hit with great force
shred (paragraph G) = cut into small pieces
puncture (paragraph G) = put a hole in something
intestines (paragraph G) = internal digestive organs
call on (paragraph I) = count on, rely on
nightmare (paragraph K) = frightening dream
rehabilitation (paragraph L) = process of recovering one's health after an illness or accident

Note that more vocabulary from the passage will be studied in exercise **B** on page 226.

IDEAS FOR . . . Checking Comprehension

Divide the class into two groups. Assign one part of the reading to each group (either "Breath of Life" or "A Survivor's Story"). Each group will prepare a summary of their section but will include three facts that aren't true. Then they will exchange their summaries. The other group will read the summary and—without looking at the book—try to identify the errors. This activity can also be done in pairs.

IDEAS FOR . . . Expansion

Ask students to research other benefits of yoga or meditation and find out how it is used in medical treatments, for example, in the treatment of post-traumatic stress disorder.

45 mins

Understanding the Reading

(pages 226–227)

Check the answers to exercise **D** on page 222.

Answer Key

control our fear, survived a life-threatening accident by controlling her fear

Exercise A. | Identifying Main Ideas

- Ask students to work individually.
- Call on students to read their answers aloud.

Answer Key

1. breathing, fear
2. alter, brain
3. control, survive
4. rescued, hospital, doctor

Exercise B. | Identifying Meaning from Context

- Ask students to work in pairs to locate and discuss the meaning in context of each word.
- Check the answers as a class.
- Ask students to make up additional sentences that illustrate the meaning of each word or phrase.

Answer Key

1. a time of danger or difficulty
2. control it
3. do something unexpected
4. push it into something very forcefully
5. return to consciousness
6. effective
7. show no emotion

TIP **Ask students to name the three most important ideas in the passage, if possible, without looking back at the reading. Then have them check the questions in exercise C to see if they are the same.**

Exercise C. | Identifying Key Details

- Allow time for students to work individually.
- Discuss the answers as a class.

Answer Key

1. She was traveling by bus, when a logging truck crashed into the bus.
2. She had studied Vipassana yoga and meditation for years.
3. a) She did a thousand sit-ups a day.
b) She climbed Mount Kilimanjaro in 2004.
c) She traveled back to Laos and rode the same bus route again in 2005.

Exercise D. | Identifying Adverbial Phrases

- Refer students back to page 220 for information about adverbial phrases.
- As you check the answers, ask students to identify whether the adverbial phases tell *when, how,* or *why.*

Answer Key

1. For most of history (when)
2. for crisis situations (why)
3. By consciously slowing down the breath (how)
4. When she compared their brain images (when)
5. With training (how)
6. Every morning (when)

Exercise E. | Critical Thinking: Understanding an Author's Purpose

Review the information in paragraphs A–E. Ask students to summarize the main points. Then discuss how these points are illustrated in Alison's story.

Answer Key

Alison used meditation to control her breathing and her fear. Because she had studied yoga and meditation for years, her brain had developed the ability to control stress.

Exercise F. | Critical Thinking: Synthesizing

- Ask students to discuss the questions in groups and then write their answers individually.
- Compare answers as a class.

Answer Key

1. They were both in extreme life-threatening situations. They both responded to fear by breathing calmly and concentrating on their thought processes.
2. Diego Asencio was not physically harmed, but Alison had severe physical injuries. Diego Asencio was captured by an armed group, but Alison was in an accident.
3. The reader would understand how the physical symptoms of fear can be consciously controlled.

45 mins

Exploring Written English

(pages 228–230)

Exercise A.

- Read the writing goal aloud.
- Explain the purpose of a descriptive narrative (to tell a story) and point out that descriptive narratives are usually told using past forms.
- Go over the information in the **Language for Writing** box. Check comprehension by asking about the use of each past form.
- Allow time for students to work individually.
- Call on students to read sentences aloud. Ask them to identify each of the past forms and to explain why they chose their answers.
- Ask general questions about the paragraph using a variety of past forms.

Answer Key

1. had just completed **2.** arrived **3.** had received
4. had been hiking **5.** had fallen **6.** was snowing
7. was making **8.** sat **9.** got **10.** had learned

Writing Skill: Planning a Descriptive Narrative

- Ask students to tell you what they think goes in each paragraph of a descriptive narrative.
- Go over the information in the **Writing Skill** box.
- Ask some comprehension questions: *What is an example of writing in the first person? What should you write in the first paragraph?*

Exercise B. | Critical Thinking: Analyzing

- Allow time for students to work in pairs.
- Discuss the answers as a class.

Answer Key

1. First person
2. The conflict is the challenge she faced in overcoming her injuries.
3. Back and ribs, arm
pulled herself out of the bus and crawled to the road
calm herself down
an aid worker, seven hours
4. She received treatment and was able to recover from her injuries.
5. When (paragraph G), Then (paragraph H), eventually (paragraph J)

Exercise C. | Beginning Your Research

You may want to brainstorm possible names of famous people that your students know about.

Exercise D. | Continuing Your Research

- Remind students of the importance of evaluating website information (see page 181 in Unit 8).
- Remind students of ways to quote or paraphrase from a source (see page 182 in Unit 8).
- Remind students to keep notes of all sources to use in their references later.

Writing Task: Drafting

(page 231)

Exercise A. | Planning

- Go over the four steps in this exercise.
- Allow time for students to complete their charts, using ideas from exercises **C** and **D** as appropriate.
- Move around the class while students are writing, offering help and advice as needed.
- Ask one or two students to read out their thesis statements.

Exercise B. | Draft 1

- As students write their first draft, walk around and offer help as needed.
- You may want to set this task for homework.

Writing Task: Revising

(pages 232–233)

Exercise C. | Critical Thinking: Analyzing

- Explain that analyzing this model essay will help students to revise their own writing.
- Allow time for students to work in pairs.
- Ask students to identify the counterarguments and evaluate the use of sources.
- Ask students what they liked or disliked in this essay. What points did they find most convincing and why?

Answer Key

1. **Thesis statement:** . . . when your situation seems hopeless, simply doing the next right thing can save your life.
2. **Survivor's name:** Michael Andereggen

   Setting: He was climbing the 11,624-foot Mount Temple in Canada's Banff National Park with his climbing partner, Kyle Smith.

   Conflict: After 18 hours of climbing, he suddenly slipped and fell 400 feet, ending up unconscious and alone in the snow.
3. **Events in the narrative:** 1. He suddenly slipped and fell 400 feet. 2. He realized that he was badly injured. 3. He realized that the best thing he could do was stay very still. 4. He found himself in wet clothes, lying in melted snow. 5. He crossed his arms over his chest to keep warm. 6. He flexed his leg muscles to keep his blood flowing. 7. He heard a faint noise in the distance. 8. He waved his arm in the direction of the sound. 9. He was so relieved that he began to sob.
4. **Summary statement:** However, by staying calm and taking simple but effective steps, he stayed alive long enough to be rescued.
5. **Resolution:** He was found by a park employee.

Exercise D. | Revising

Ask students to reread their work carefully and look for ways to improve it.

Exercise E. | Peer Evaluation

- Explain that this process will help students to see if they have organized and expressed their ideas clearly.
- Discuss the four steps in the evaluation process to make sure students know what to do.
- Ensure that both members of the pair have equal time to give feedback.

Exercise F. | Draft 2

Walk around and monitor students as they work. Provide assistance as needed.

Writing Task: Editing

(page 234)

Exercise G. | Editing Practice

- Go over the information in the box.
- Allow time for students to find and correct the mistakes.
- Invite volunteers to read out and explain the corrected sentences.

Answer Key

1. Asencio **was** at a party at the Dominican Republic's embassy when rebels attacked it.
2. The rebels began firing in the air and at security guards. During the gunfight, Asencio **hid** between a sofa and a wall.
3. As soon as he heard the first gunshot, Asencio's body **started** to react.
4. Asencio's body had an instinctive fear reaction. His blood changed, his heart rate **increased**, and his body filled up with chemicals such as cortisol and adrenaline.
5. Twelve more rebels entered the embassy after the first four **started** firing their guns.

Exercise H. | Editing Checklist

- Read the sentences in the Editing Checklist.
- Allow time for students to read and edit their work.

Exercise I. | Final Draft

- Allow time for students to work on their final draft (or set this for homework).
- Collect their work.

IDEAS FOR . . . Expansion

Ask students to write about a personal experience of overcoming a problem or an obstacle. What was the problem? What was difficult about it? What helped them to overcome it? What lesson did they learn from this experience?

Ask students to research and choose two people who have overcome adversity to become a famous athlete, writer, singer, musician, actor, or artist. What do these two people have in common? What helped them to become successful?

Social Relationships

Complete the chart as you read *Gender in the Wild.*

	Animal Species	Country	Behavior Observed in Females	Behavior Observed in Males	Conclusions
1			Female elephants cooperate to ____________.	Male elephants were thought to be ____________. Now researchers have found that ____________.	Hierarchies help to ____________.
2					
3					

Extension	What other animal species have social hierarchies?

Science and Detection

Complete the flowcharts as you read *King Tut's Family Secrets.*

What technology was used?	→	What was discovered?	→	What was the conclusion?
1. CT scan of Tutankhamun's mummy	→	hole in skull was not cause of death	→	made during mummification process
2. ____________	→	____________	→	____________
3. ____________	→	____________	→	____________
4. ____________	→	____________	→	____________
5. ____________	→	____________	→	____________

Extension	What other historical artifact or mystery was solved using technology?

City Solutions

Complete the diagram as you read *Living on an Urban Planet.*

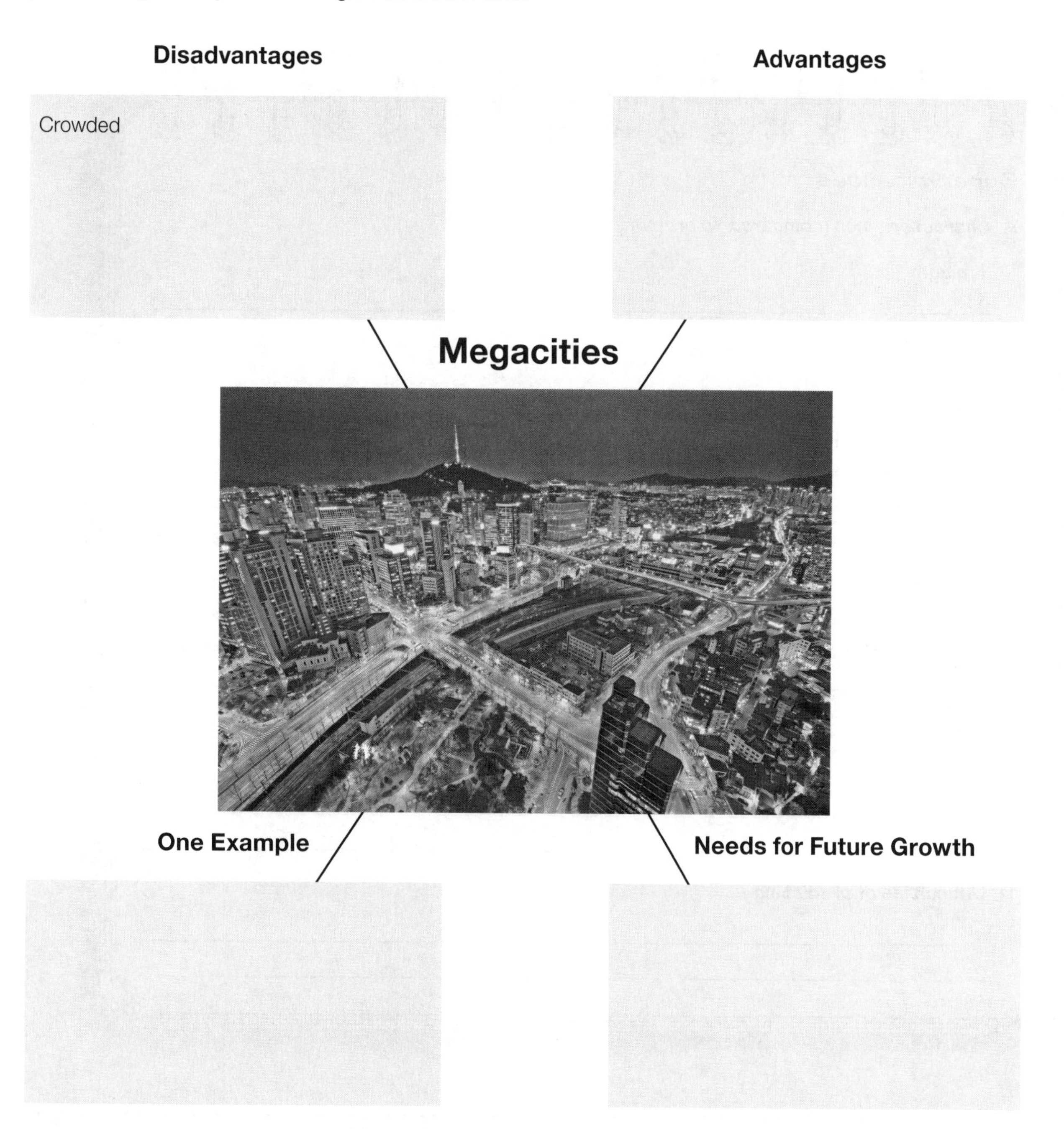

Extension	What other ideas for improving modern city living do you know about?

Danger Zones

Complete the outline as you read *Yellowstone's Smoking Bomb.*

Supervolcanoes

A. Characteristics (compared to ordinary volcanoes)

1. bigger
2. ____________________
3. ____________________

B. Formation

1. intense heat pushes up
2. melts rock and ____________________
3. chamber fills with ____________________
4. ____________________ forms a dome
5. ____________________
6. ____________________ through the cracks
7. ____________________ is emptied
8. ____________________

C. Effects

1. gases ____________________
2. ____________________ creates a haze
3. causes ____________________

D. Difficulties of predicting

1. ____________________
2. ____________________

Extension	What are some other places with volcanoes? What facts do you know about them?

The Business of Tourism

Complete the chart as you read *Geotourism in Action: Three Success Stories.*

Tourism	 Ecuador	 Nepal	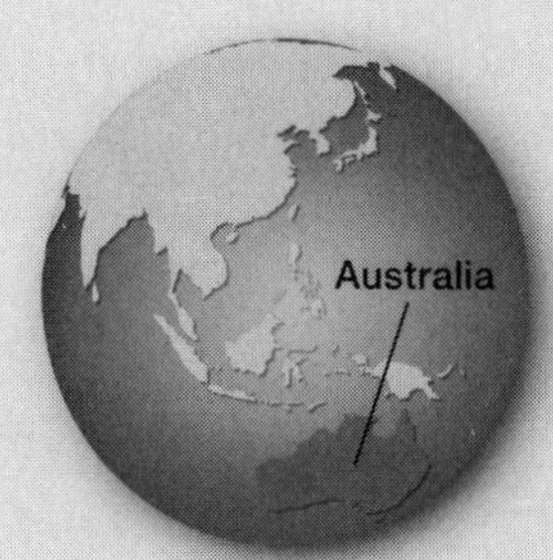 Australia
How it helps the community	*Tourism provides an income for local people.*		
How it helps the environment			
How it empowers people			

Extension	What similar programs do you know about in your country or elsewhere?

Landscape and Imagination

Complete the chart as you read *The Poet of the Outback.*

How did Paterson get the idea for "Waltzing Matilda"?	
What are the characteristics of the poem?	
Why do you think it became so popular?	
Why is Paterson's work important to Australians?	

Extension	What similar poem or book do you know about in your language or in English?

Global Appetites

Complete the diagram as you read *Eight Steps toward a Sustainable Future.* Write notes to summarize each step.

Introduction	→	Earth's population is growing—need to conserve energy and consume less
1. Sustainable Communities	→	
2. Safer Livestock Production	→	
3. Renewable Energy Resources	→	
4. Socially Responsible Investing	→	
5. Greener Lightbulbs	→	
6. Certified Forests	→	
7. Green Employment	→	
8. Lower Carbon Emissions	→	

Extension	What other steps toward a sustainable future do you know about?

Medical Innovators

Complete the chart as you read *Pioneers of Medicine.*

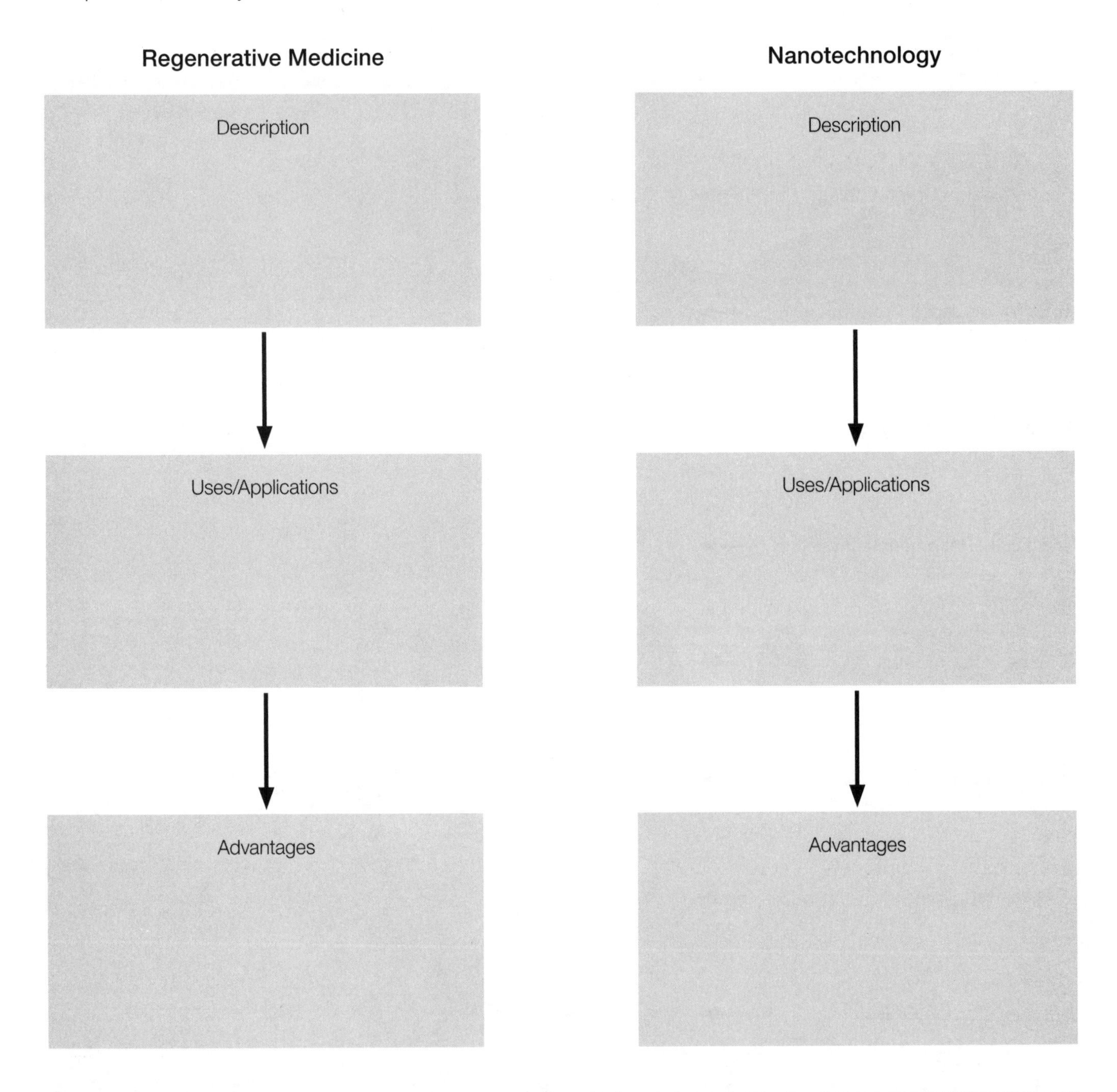

Extension	What other recent developments in medicine do you know about?

World Languages

Complete the chart as you read *Vanishing Voices.*

Facts about world languages	
Why are some languages disappearing?	

Examples		
Language	Country	Unique Words or Ideas

Organizations Trying to Save Languages	
Name	Methods

Extension	What other languages spoken by very few people do you know about?

Survival Instinct

Complete the timeline as you read *A Survivor's Story*.

January 2000 ↓	Alison was ______________ when it was struck by a ______________. She pushed __________ and __________ and __________ onto the road. She focused ______________________________________.
A few hours later ↓	
4 months later ↓	
2004 ↓	
2005 ↓	
Now	

Extension	What other facts do you know about how to survive in extreme situations—for example, a shark attack, an earthquake, etc.?